MICHAEL JACKSON'S

CONCISE MALT WHISKY
COMPANION

SPECIAL EDITION

MICHAEL JACKSON'S

CONCISE MALT WHISKY
COMPANION

SPECIAL EDITION

LONDON • NEW YORK • MUNICH
MELBOURNE • DELHI

RESEARCH
Owen D. L. Barstow and Cathy Turner

PHOTOGRAPHY
Steve Gorton and Ian O'Leary

ADDITIONAL MATERIAL
Dave Broom, Jürgen Deibel, and Martine Nouet

For Dorling Kindersley

PROJECT ART EDITOR Sara Robin	**EXECUTIVE MANAGING EDITOR** Adèle Hayward
MANAGING ART EDITOR Nick Harris	**PRODUCTION CONTROLLER** Rebecca Short

DTP DESIGNER
Traci Salter

Produced for Dorling Kindersley by

cobaltid

The Stables, Wood Farm, Deopham Road,
Attleborough, Norfolk NR17 1AJ
www.cobaltid.co.uk

ART EDITORS	**EDITORS**
Paul Reid	Marek Walisiewicz
Lloyd Tilbury	Maddy King

Fifth Edition published 2004 by Dorling Kindersley Limited
This abridged and revised edition published 2006 by Dorling Kindersley

The Penguin Group

2 4 6 8 10 9 7 5 3 1

ISBN-13 9-7814-0532-134-1

ISBN-10 1-4053-2134-2

Colour reproduction by Colourscan, Singapore
Printed in China by L-Res
Discover more at
www.dk.com

CONTENTS

Before dinner or after? With coffee, chocolate, or a cigar? These are just some of the moments for malt. There are suggestions with every entry ...

JOHNNIE BE GOOD

Striding like a giant from billboards on the most prime of sites, the colourful and energetic figure of Johnnie Walker always seemed like a character in a national tableau. Surely he is: symbolising good cheer. When we say that someone is a legend, what exactly do we mean? That he is a myth, an invention? Or that he is so real as to be larger than life? An advertising agency can devise and sustain a myth, but Johnnie Walker was a real person. He was one of the Scottish giants who transformed a rustic sideline into the most cosmopolitan of drinks. This was achieved by the magic of blending: the rounding of the wilder flavours and the leavening with lighter grain whiskies.

It is often assumed that Blended Scotches offer the easiest route to a taste for whisky, and that malts come later. That was not my experience. I began to appreciate blends after first gaining a knowledge of their component malts – I was introduced to malt whisky by a fellow journalist in Edinburgh. Nor do I agree with the popular view that Blended Scotch Whiskies are always lighter in character than Single Malts. Some blends are, indeed, very light in flavour, others more robust. The same is true of malts. Some blends aim for a perfect balance, like an orchestra where strings, woodwind, and brass are so melded that they can barely be distinguished. I prefer the orchestration where the sections and the soloists are clearly identifiable. A good example, in my view, is Johnnie Walker Black Label, where the grain whiskies provide a bright background, against which the more vividly individualistic malts can be highlighted. While I avoid naming favourites, on the basis that there are different whiskies for every mood and moment, I am on record as especially enjoying Johnnie Walker Black: as piquant and peppery as hot-and-sour soup or New Orleans gumbo; as robust as rock and roll. No need to urge Johnnie to be good, as Chuck Berry did. Johnnie Walker Black is always beautiful.

Another treat, when I am feeling in expansive mood, is Johnnie Walker Blue. It has the appropriately bluesey sophistication and maturity of the later Sinatra. Some whiskies inspire culinary comparisons; others evoke music. There are whiskies that punch like

Marciano and others that dance like Muhammad Ali. Having so enjoyed the Johnnie Walker Blended Scotches, I was delighted when I was asked to taste Green Label Blended Malt. How does it perform among the Single Malts? This Concise Edition of my tasting notes will tell you that and much more. Descriptors for Green Label? "Sporting" and "Generous" come to mind.

The differences in character between one whisky and another have always fascinated me. In trying better to understand this, I began 30 years ago by reading authors such as Barnard, Bruce Lockhart, Daiches, Gunn, and McDowell. They told me about the process of whisky making, its lore, history, and geography, but little about aroma or taste. At that time, malt whisky was very much a local drink in the Highlands. Scotland's great national drink was almost a secret.

I had written the odd short piece on the subject in the 1970s, but started more serious research in the 1980s. In those earliest days, my questions about single malts were not welcomed by some of the more conservative souls in the industry. Malt whisky, in their view, belonged only in blends. Their myopia was perhaps forgivable: blended Scotch whisky was the world's most popular drink, and its sales were built on brand loyalty. Attempts to describe aromas and flavours and explore connoisseurship might unsettle such loyalties. This was whisky, not wine or food.

Writing on whisky was a lonely business, but I was given great encouragement by Wallace Milroy and Derek Cooper. My first book on the subject was The World Guide to Whisky, published in 1987, and this was quickly followed by my malt whisky book in 1989.

No other writer had attempted so thoroughly to describe the taste of individual whiskies, discussed so many, or taken the controversial step of scoring them. In that first edition, there were fewer than 250 tasting notes. By the fourth edition, the tally had gone past 750; in the fifth edition, I exceeded 1,000. If the tireless (not to say immortal) Johnnie Walker is to lead a new fashion for Blended Malts, I may have to find myself a bigger tasting room.

Michael Jackson

THE ORIGINS OF
MALT WHISKY

WHILE GRAPE VINES HAVE their roots in prehistory, barley staked out the beginning of civilization. As hunter-gatherers, human beings picked wild fruits such as grapes, but this source of refreshment and nutrition had a short season and a propensity to rot (or spontaneously ferment) into wines. Fruits take up rainfall from the soil and turn it into highly fermentable, sugary juice. Wild yeasts trigger fermentation, and this process creates alcohol. Perhaps the hunter-gatherers enjoyed the effect, but wine did not provide them with any much needed protein.

When human beings ceased to be nomadic and settled in organized societies they did so in order to cultivate crops. The earliest evidence of this, between 13,000 and 8000 years ago, occurs at several sites in the fertile crescent of the Middle East. The first crop was a prototype barley, and the first explanation of its use is a depiction in Sumerian clay tablets of beer making. This is sometimes described as the world's first recipe of any kind.

HALF-WAY TO WHISKY

To grow barley, transform it into malt and then into beer, is half-way towards the making of whisky. While it is easy to obtain the sugars from fruit – peel me a grape, take a bite from an apple – grain is less yielding. The first step toward the unlocking of the sugars in barley and several other grains is the process of malting. This means that the grain is steeped in water, partially germinated, and then dried. The Sumerian civilization was on land that is today Iraq. It may be that malting occurred naturally while the barley was still in the field, as the water rose and fell in the flood plains of this land. This is described poetically on clay tablets in "A Hymn to Ninkasi" *(see p. 26).*

It seems likely that at this stage the Sumerians had no more precise aim than to make grain edible. They did so in the form of beer, though pictograms and relics suggest a grainy, porridgey beverage consumed through straws. This depiction bears a startling resemblance to the "traditional" beer still brewed in villages in some parts of Africa.

Road to the Isles
A few miles from the Bushmills distillery in Ireland, this remarkable rock formation heads for Fingal's Cave, Staffa, and Mull. The first whisky road … or the first whisky legend?

> WHEN YOU POUR OUT THE FILTERED
> BEER OF THE COLLECTOR VAT,
> IT IS [LIKE] THE ONRUSH OF TIGRIS AND EUPHRATES.
> NINKASI, YOU ARE THE ONE WHO POURS OUT THE
> FILTERED BEER OF THE COLLECTOR VAT,
> IT IS [LIKE] THE ONRUSH OF TIGRIS AND EUPHRATES.
>
> **Grain and water meet ...**
>
> *... in the "Hymn to Ninkasi" (c. 1800bc), found on tablets at several sites in Iraq.*
> *Translated in 1964, by Miguel Civil, of the Oriental Institute of the University of Chicago.*
> *The first evidence of malting?*

If the cultivation of grain originally radiated from the first civilization of the Ancient World, the crop itself varied from place to place. To the east, the Chinese and Japanese grow rice, which is fermented to produce saké. To the north, the Russians use rye to make kvass. To the west, barley is brewed. The words "brewed" and "bread" have the same etymology, and, in Germany, beer is sometimes known as "liquid bread".

The soft, sensuous, delicate, capricious grape and the tall, spiky, resilient grain compete to make the world's greatest drinks: fermented and distilled. The weather divides temperate Europe into wine and beer belts. Wine is made in the grape-growing south: Greece, Italy, France, Iberia. Beer belongs to the grainy north: the Czech Republic, Germany, Belgium, and the British Isles. All of these countries also produce distilled counterparts, but the real emphasis on spirits is in the colder countries. The spirits belt links Russia, Poland, the Baltic and Nordic states, and Scotland.

Modern-day Iraq is due south of Armenia, and the Greek historian Herodotus tells us that the Armenians made "barley water". So perhaps the brewing of barley malt spread by way of Armenia, Georgia, and the Ukraine. The Greeks also called all "strangers" Celts. The Romans called them Gallic people, and a part of Turkey is known as Galatia. The term "Galatian" was also used by the Roman author Columella to describe the two-row "race" of barley, preferred today by many brewers.

Sites that were Celtic settlements are even today known for the brewing of beer, notably sites in Bohemia, Bavaria, and Belgium. Many of these sites later gave rise to abbeys, with breweries. Most of the early brewing sites in England, Scotland, and Ireland are on the locations of former abbeys. So are the distilling towns of Cork and Midleton in Ireland. The northeast of Ireland and the western isles of Scotland have associations with St Columba, who urged his community of Iona to grow barley. In 1494, Friar Cor, of Lindores Abbey in Fife, placed on record in the rolls of the Scottish Exchequer the purchase of malt "to make *aqua vitae*". He probably wasn't the first malt distiller, but he left us the first evidence.

THE ART OF DISTILLATION

It is easy to see how spontaneous fermentation provides a natural model for the first brewers. Evaporation and condensation occur in nature, too, but it is not clear when, or where, distillation was first practised. To distil is to boil the water, wine, or beer, collect the steam, and condense it back into liquid. This drives off certain substances (for example, the salt in water) and concentrates others (such as the alcohol in wine or beer). The process was used by Phoenician sailors to render sea water drinkable, by alchemists, by makers of perfumes and, eventually, in the production of medicines and alcoholic drinks.

One theory has the Phoenicians bringing distillation to Western Europe, via the Mediterranean and Spain, whence it crossed the sea again to Ireland. Another theory has the art spreading by way of Russia and the Nordic countries to Scotland.

The fermented raw material – wine or beer – is boiled to make steam, which, being wraith-like, may have given rise to the English word "spirit" or to the German "*Geist*" (ghost), especially since condensation brings it back to life in a restored (and restorative) form. The "water of life" they call it: vodka, a diminutive form, in Slavic countries; aquavit, in various spellings, in Nordic lands; *eau-de-vie* in French; and *usquebaugh*, in various spellings, in Gaelic. This last became *usky*, then whisky, in English. All of these terms at first simply indicated a distillate, made from whatever was local.

All spirit drinks were originally made in a batch process in a vessel that superficially resembles a kettle or cooking pot, and malt whisky is still made in this way today. But this "pot still" was an inefficient purification vessel, and, in the early days, if the spirit emerged with flavours that were considered disagreeable, they were masked with spices, berries, and fruits.

"PLAIN MALT"

In the mid-1700s, a distinction was made in Scotland between flavoured spirits and "plain malt". As the first industrial nation, Britain shaped its beer and whisky with the early technologies of the Industrial Revolution: England's "bright beer" was a copper-coloured pale ale, rather than the more "evolved" golden lager of Continental Europe, which was made using more advanced techniques. Scotland's whisky remained a pot-still product, with its own inherent flavours, turned to an attractive complexity.

Most of the northern European countries use a generic term such as "schnapps" for a spirit, and offer both plain and flavoured examples. More specific flavourings include caraway and dill, traditional in the aquavit of Scandinavia; and juniper, together with botanical flavourings such as iris root and citrus peel, in the gins of northern Germany, the Low Countries, northern France, and England. Flavoured or not, many grain-based spirits outside Britain employ a column still, and most are not aged.

The elements that go to make up a Scottish malt whisky are the local water; a grist comprising malted barley only; traditionally, a degree of peat; pot stills, usually designed and built in Scotland; and ageing in oak casks. The last of these elements gradually became more significant from the late 1700s onwards.

BLENDED SCOTCH

Like most drinks production, the distilling of malt whisky in Scotland was originally a sideline for farmers. In the coastal coves and Highland glens, illicit distillation was rife. Legislation in 1824 to regulate this activity began the shaping of today's industry. That process was largely finished by the legislation of 1909–15, which initially arose from a trading standards case in the London borough of Islington.

For the farmer-distiller, a few casks of malt whisky might be a hedge against a rainy day. A farm distillery would not have a bottling line. The casks could be sold directly to wealthy householders, to hotels or pubs, or to a licensed grocer, a Scottish institution similar to an

A fair copita
At the Talisker distillery, on the Isle of Skye, Graham Logie monitors the progress of maturing whisky. In his left hand is a valinch (also known as a thief), the tool used to withdraw a sample from the cask. In his right hand, a copita tasting glass. The vital instrument is his nose. Will the whisky meet other malts behind the Green Label?

American country store. (The outstanding example of such a shop, and still active, is Gordon & MacPhail of Elgin.) One or two renowned distillers might sell their whisky to a wine merchant, sometimes as far away as Edinburgh or London.

Each farmer's whisky would vary from one year to the next, and supply would be irregular. So rather than run out of farmer McSporran's fine dram, the licensed grocers would vat the malts and sell the result under their own label. Some became famous: names such as Johnnie Walker, Chivas Brothers, and George Ballantine. Among the wine merchants known for their bottlings, two in London are still active: Justerini & Brooks and Berry Brothers & Rudd.

Vatting turned to blending when, in the mid-1800s, the column-shaped continuous still was patented. This type of still, operated on an industrial scale, can produce whisky that is lighter in flavour and body. It can also produce whisky more quickly, at a lower cost, and in larger quantities than a pot still. Column-still whisky provides the bulk of a blend, while a combination of pot-still malt whiskies add character and individuality. The volume afforded by blended Scotches, and their less challenging style, helped them become the world's most popular spirits at a time when much of the globe was embraced by the British Empire.

Mountainous Scotland, with its long coastline, had provided mariners, explorers, engineers, teachers, soldiers, and administrators for the empire. Each turned out also to be a propagandist for the virtues of his country's greatest product.

BORN-AGAIN MALTS

More than 90 per cent of malt whisky still goes into blends. Scotland has about 100 malt distilleries, of which about two thirds are working at any one time. All but a handful are owned by international drinks companies whose products include blended Scotches. A blend can contain anything from six or seven malts to 30 or 40. The drinks companies like to own the distilleries whose malt whiskies are vital to their blends. They also exchange malts with one another.

The big drinks companies have been growing through mergers since the 1920s. A round of mergers after the Second World War left the handful of remaining independent distillers feeling vulnerable. William Grant & Sons, producers of Glenfiddich and Balvenie, decided they no longer wished to rely on supplying blenders, but to actively market their whisky as a single malt. The industry view was that single malts belonged to the past, and that the dominant position of the blends could not be challenged. Happily, Grant's were not dissuaded.

FLAVOURS

THE INFLUENCE OF THE LANDSCAPE

THE UNIVERSE OF SPIRITS BEGAN to change when the word "designer", having become an adjective, attached itself to the word "vodka". Then, some of the most famous names in the world of distillation became better known for their "ready-to-drink" confections, misleadingly known in the United States as "malternatives". Now a new generation of consumers faces a choice between drinks that come from nowhere, taste of nothing much, and have a logo for a name; and drinks that come from somewhere, have complex aromas and flavours, and may have a name that is hard to pronounce.

Such drinks reflect their place of origin. They have evolved. They have a story to tell. They are good company, and they require something of the drinker in return: that he or she experiences the pleasure of learning to drink. Real, evolved drinks begin as the gift of God. They are grown, whether from grapes, grain, sugar cane, or, for example, the agave plant. They arise from their own *terroir*: geology, soil, vegetation, topography, weather, water, and air. To what extent they are influenced by each of these elements is a matter for debate, often passionate. People care about real drinks.

The most sophisticated of real drinks are the brandies of France and the whiskies of the British Isles. The most complex brandies are the cognacs and armagnacs. The most complex whiskies are those of Scotland and Ireland.

Within these two duopolies, cognac and Scotch are the best known. In Cognac, the regions of production are contiguous, stretch about 144 kilometres (90 miles) from one end to the other, and are all in flat countryside. The whisky distilleries of Scotland are spread over an area of about 448 kilometres (280 miles) from one end of the country to the other, from the Lowlands to the northern Highlands, from mountain to shore, and from the Hebrides in the west to Orkney (and by now Shetland?) in the north. Theirs is surely the greater complexity.

Under the volcano
Scotland's landscape can be silent and still, yet the evidence of eruptions, glaciations, and rocky collisions is everywhere. The dews and frosts, the marine plants and mountain forests – each valley or island has its own flavour. Arran, left, has extinct volcanoes and a newish distillery.

Whisky is a real drink. A single malt is as real as it gets. There are many potential influences on its character, and much dispute as to the relative importance – if any – of each: the variety of barley; the strains of yeast; the size of still; and the provenance of the casks.

On these and other issues ever more research is carried out, but an apparent insight into one stage of the whisky-making process may raise new questions about the next. In production, if a procedure is changed, the result may not be apparent until the whisky is mature, perhaps 10 years hence.

THE WHISKY COUNTRIES

Scotland and Ireland can be cool and rainy, but their climates are temperate. The conditions are very favourable for the growing of barley, though excessive damp and wind can occasionally be a problem.

The windy main island of the Orkney islands still cultivates bere, a precursor to barley, but grown today for local bakers rather than distillers. It was used in whisky making in the past, and its importance was such that a dispute over taxes on bere even threatened the Act of Union in 1707.

Today, just as different wine regions champion their own grapes, so there are debates in Europe as to the merits of "continental" barleys, such as those grown in Moravia, Bohemia, and Bavaria, versus the "maritime" examples of Denmark, Scotland, England, and Ireland.

The blood of …
… John Barleycorn was spilled by Robert Burns, a Lowlander but from the West. This field of barley is in the East, near the Lowland distillery, Glenkinchie.

Supporters of the continental barleys say they provide a sweeter, nuttier flavour. Protagonists for the maritime varieties argue that they have a clean, "sea-breeze" character.

Naturally, the Scots prefer their own barley. Depending upon the harvest, and their own needs, they have on occasion exported, but in other periods they have augmented their own malt with "imports" from England. Their second choice would be Denmark, and then elsewhere. Purists would prefer that the Scots used only their own barley. The Scots could argue that they are simply victims of their own success in selling so much of their whisky.

It is because barley is more resilient that it has a broader belt of cultivation, and can be more easily transported, than the grapes that make wine and brandy. Scotland's main growing regions are on the more sheltered eastern side of the country: on the shores of the Moray firth (The Black Isle and The Laich of Moray), Aberdeenshire, and the Borders. Ireland's are in the southeast, behind an imaginary line on the map, which runs from the border city of Dundalk (with a history of brewing) in County Louth, to the sailing (and gastronomic) resort of Kinsale, County Cork. Both countries might wish for more cultivable land; Scotland is mountainous, and Ireland boggy.

TASTING THE *TERROIR*

Scotland seems like a machine for the making of whisky: a nation on a small island, awaiting the vapours of the sea; providing summits to unlock their precipitation, which then filters through a diversity of rock, via springs and mountain streams, over peat and heather, to the fields of barley and the distilleries.

Scotland's heather-clad hillsides, its peaty moorlands, and its seaweed-fringed islands all contribute to the character of its national drink. To sample some of the more pungent malts is to taste the *terroir*. But to what extent are the aromas and flavours carried by the mountain streams or burns that feed the distilleries? Is the greater influence in the peat that is used to dry the malt? Then there is the question of the atmosphere in the damp, earth-floored warehouses, and its influence on the whisky.

Heather, peat, and seaweed are not unique to Scotland, but the country is unusually rich in all three. Their local variations, their proportion, their juxtaposition, and their relationship with the rest of the landscape are unique. Every landscape is. The colour of a person's hair or eyes, or the shape of a nose or jawline, are not unique, but the face is, and it derives from them all.

On the map, Scotland presents a weatherbeaten face. The outline – the coast – is penetrated by endless inlets from the sea. These inlets are variously known as "sea lochs" or "firths"; the latter word has the same roots as the Norwegian "fjord".

"SCANDINAVIAN SCOTLAND"

In its topography, its use of Viking words, its Protestant rigour (with some ambivalence toward alcohol), Scotland can resemble Norway, the nearest of the Scandinavian countries. Scotland seems to reach northwards, higher into the spirits belt, while its Celtic cousin Ireland (more especially the Republic) appears to lean south, toward the Roman Catholic countries of mainland Europe.

Scotland is bigger in both land area and population than Ireland. It also has 20 or 30 times as many distilleries. At one stage, for a brief period, the numbers of stills in each of the countries were close, but Ireland's industry spent decades in decline before rediscovering itself in recent years. Whichever country "discovered" the barley distillate, and this is contentious, Scotland is today's pre-eminent "Land of Whisky".

Only whisky made there can be called Scotch. For many years, the industry repeated this without making clear its meaning. Were their spokesmen simply repeating an appellation? Or did they mean that no other country could make a comparable product? Scotch whiskies all taste of their homeland to varying degrees, but in many the taste is so subtle as to be scarcely evident, while in others the aromas of peat and seaweed, for example, are wonderfully shocking.

The handful of malt whiskies (as opposed to the "pot-still Irish" type) made at Bushmills and Cooley in Ireland are similar in style to their Scottish counterparts; as are the handful of Japanese malts, though some have distinct local features. But a whisky cannot taste of Scotland if it is made in Ireland or Japan, however similar the *terroir*. The most characterful whiskies taste of the *terroir*, wherever it is. They are real drinks.

ROCK

Geology as a discipline began in Scotland – with the book *Theory of the Earth*, published in 1788. The author, Dr James Hutton, was a Scot, inspired in part by the natural landscape of his homeland. The geology of Scotland is more varied than that of any country of a similar size. Much of this diversity arises from a spectacular collision 400–500 million years ago. The part of the earth's crust that is now Scotland was at that time attached to North America. It was in

Rosebank
*Roses once bloomed
at Rosebank. Now
rosebay willowherb
has taken over.
The whisky tastes
of camomile ... or
carboniferous rock.*

collision with a European plate that included England, Wales, and
Ireland. The fault line where the two plates met was more or less
followed a few million years later by Hadrian's Wall, and the border
between England and Scotland has rarely strayed more than a few
kilometres from this line since. The geological turbulence continued,
with everything from volcanoes to glaciers, until 20,000 years ago.

Thus not only did geology begin with Scotland, but Scotland began
with geology: with the thrusts, intrusions, eruptions, and glaciations. It
came to rest, semantically, as a Gaelic-language landscape, with
"corries" (hollows in the mountainside); "lochans" (small lakes) and
"lochs" in a wide range of sizes (sometimes stretching for many miles,
and possibly with a small opening to the sea); "straths" (broad valleys);
and the "glens" (or narrower valleys) that appear on every other label.
This is the whisky-making machine.

In 1990, geologists Stephen Cribb and Julie Davison made a study
of rock formations in Scotland's whisky regions, and compared them
with tasting notes in books on the drink, including this one. Their
findings suggested that the similar tastes in certain whiskies produced
near each other might in part be due to the similar rock from which
the water rose. For example, in the Lowlands, the crisp, dry
Glenkinchie and Rosebank share the same carboniferous rock. The
oldest rock is that which supplies water to the Caol Ila, Bowmore and
Bruichladdich distilleries on Islay, off the west coast of Scotland; it was
formed about 600–800 million years ago, and seems to contribute an
iron-like flavour.

For many years, whisky makers always spoke of granite. Being so
hard, granite does not donate minerals to the water. Thus hard rock
means soft water, and vice versa. Granite is the principal rock of the

Grampians, the group of mountains and sub-ranges that dominates the Highlands, and from which the River Spey flows. Every Speyside distiller seemed to claim that he had soft water, "rising from granite and flowing over peat". In looking at the Grampians, the Cribbs' book *Whisky on the Rocks* identified Ben Rinnes and the Conval Hills as sources of the typical Speyside water, feeding distilleries such as Dufftown, Aberlour, and Craigellachie. The study went on to point out that the region's geology is diverse, embracing substantial areas of limestone and sandstone. One distillery that has, sensibly, made a virtue of its sandstone water source is Glenmorangie, located in the northern Highlands.

Mineral flavours – and textures – are familiar from bottled waters, and also seem evident in some malt whiskies. Water is used to steep the grain at maltings (though only a handful of these are attached to distilleries). It is employed in the mash tun at every distillery to extract the sugars from the malted barley. It is used to reduce the strength of spirit in the cask to aid maturation. It is also used to reduce mature whisky to bottling strength. For this last stage the local water is influential only in the handful of distilleries that bottle on site, and in those cases, it is very influential indeed.

SNOW

Vodka marketeers love to promote their products with suggestions of snowy purity, whether they are distilled in St Petersburg, Poznan, or in Peoria, Illinois. Some vodkas are distilled in one place and rectified in another. Others have Slavic origins, but are produced under licence in North America or elsewhere.

Snow on the Spey
The river Spey rises south of the Dalwhinnie distillery, one of Scotland's highest. Clearly whisky made from snowmelt, but also with some peaty complexity. Absolut Scotland ...

Snow-melt is more reliably found in Scottish malt whisky. There is typically snow on Scotland's highest mountain, Ben Nevis (measuring 1344 metres or 4410 feet high), for six to seven months of the year, and occasionally for longer: perhaps from September to May, or even all year. The same can be true in the Grampians, though three or four months is more common.

At sea level, especially in the drier east, Scotland may have less than 800 millimetres (32 inches) of rain and snow a year. In the mountains, that figure can more than triple. Once the snow melts, it descends by a variety of routes, filtering through fissures in the rock, emerging from springs, swelling streams or burns, or gushing into rivers like the Spey, Livet, and Fiddich.

High in the hills, distilleries like Dalwhinnic or Braeval might regard their water as snow-melt. By the time it has swollen the Spey, then been tapped by Tamdhu, it is regarded as river water. If it filters through the Conval Hills in search of Glenfiddich, Balvenie, or Kininvie, it emerges as the spring water of Robbie Dubh. Every distillery knows where it collects its water, and protects its source as a critical asset. Distillers know where their water arrives, but it may be impossible to say whence it came, or how long its journey was, except that it was once rain or snow.

WATER

The worry over water concerns not only quality, but also quantity. A great deal is required, not only for the steeps at the maltings and the mash tun at the distillery, but also to cool the condensers or worm tubs, to wash vessels, and to reduce the strength of the spirit in the cask or the mature whisky at bottling.

Unlike brewers of beer, the distillers of whisky do not add or remove salts to change the composition of their water. Not only must water for malting and mashing be available in volume, it must also be consistent in character. If a source threatens to run dry in the summer, the distillery may stop production and devote a few weeks' "silent season" to annual maintenance and vacations. If the water runs unusually slowly, or quickly, it may become muddy or sandy. If the water source is endangered by a project in the next county upstream, that could be a critical problem. And it is certainly critical if the distillery's production is outstripping the water source. Even the most sophisticated of distillery companies has been known to hire a water diviner to find an additional nearby source. Every effort will be made to match the character of the principal water used.

The issue of soft water versus hard goes beyond the flavour of any salts naturally occurring in the water. Calcium, for example, increases the extract of malt sugars in the mash tun, and may also make for a cleaner, drier whisky. Whether it does – whether, indeed, such influences could survive distillation – is hotly debated.

Visitors to distilleries are sometimes invited to sample the water. It can taste intensely peaty. Yet the whisky may be barely peaty at all. This is the case at the famous Speyside distillery, Glen Grant. The explanation would seem to be that the peaty taste does not survive distillation. Speyside is also rich in heather. Is that why its whiskies are so floral? The circumstantial evidence is strong, but some distillers might argue that the flowery character actually results from reactions during maturation.

On the island of Islay, even the tap water can be tinged a peaty brown or ironstone red. Perhaps the water flowed over peat for a longer distance. Did it linger, and take up more peatiness? Or flow faster and dig up its peaty bed? The bed may also have contributed some ironstone, or some green, ferny, vegetal character. This time, the flavours do seem to carry over into the whisky. Perhaps the flavours were absorbed when the peaty water was used to steep the barley at the beginning of the malting process. Unlike the maltings on the mainland, those on Islay highlight the intensity of local peat. It is the use of peat fires in the drying of the grains that imparts the greatest degree of smokiness and "Islay character" to the malt. The peat in the kiln is the smoking gun. The Islay distiller has the soul of an outlaw.

PEAT

Not only is aroma the bigger part of taste – the drinks and foods that arouse the appetite and the imagination are often fragrant – but these same foods are in fact frequently grilled, barbecued, roasted, toasted, or smoked: the breakfast kippers, bacon, toast, and coffee; the steak sizzling on a

Tasting the *terroir*
The basis of terroir *is the earth. Here, it is sliced, and placed on a fire, so that its smoke pervades the malt. Some peat cutting on Islay is still done by hand.*

charcoal grill; the chestnuts roasting on an open fire. Of all the techniques historically used to kiln malt in different parts of Europe, the peat fires of Scotland surely produce the most evocative aromas. While some devotees of single malts have a catholic view, many take sides: will it be the peaty, briny whiskies of the islands and coasts; or the flowery, honeyed, sometimes sherried Speysiders?

The partisans for peat lust for its intensity (and love quoting ppm), but it also imparts a number of complex flavours and aromas. At least 80 aroma compounds have been found in peated malt.

While peatiness excites connoisseurs, it can alienate first-time tasters. When people say they "don't like" Scotch whisky, they often refer to a "funny taste", which turns out to mean peat. To take exception to such a fundamental element of the drink may seem odd, but distinctive, powerful flavours, especially if they are dry, can be challenging. Very hoppy beers are a perfect parallel. At a pinch, heavily oaked wines might also be drawn into the discussion.

In whisky, the dryness of peat provides a foil for the sweetness of barley malt, but that is a bonus, as is peat's rich content of anti-oxidants, the enemy of free radicals.

Peat was used in the first place because it is a convenient and plentiful fuel. Ninety per cent of the world's peat bogs are in temperate-to-cold parts of the northern hemisphere. Two-thirds of Britain's bogland is in Scotland, which in land area is half the size of England. Scotland's northern Highlands has Europe's largest expanse of blanket bogs. These bogs, in the counties of Caithness and Sutherland, are said to set a standard in the worldwide study of the phenomenon.

The peat that seduces whisky lovers is on the distillery islands of Orkney and Islay. In both cases, the sea air and high winds add salty flavours to the peat. The coast of Islay is heavily fringed with seaweed, which adds an iodine, medicinal character to the atmosphere. This, too, penetrates the peat. The Orcadian peat is younger, more heathery, and incorporates a wide range of salt-tolerant maritime plants. In the western islands, especially Islay, the peat is rich in bog myrtle (*Myrica gale*), also known as sweet gale, which has a sweet, cypress-like aroma and bitter flavour. Bog myrtle was one of the flavourings used in beer before the hop plant was adopted, and clearly influences the flavours imparted by the peat.

When peat is being cut by hand, the spade digs out a cube with surfaces as shiny and dark as a bar of "black" chocolate. It sometimes looks as edible as Mississippi mud pie. A closer look at the muddy block sometimes reveals the fossil-like remains of mosses. The principal component is sphagnum, a spongy moss that intertwines with other plants to form a fibrous soil, which, under pressure, will eventually become coal. The peatbogs of Scotland began to grow between 7000 and 3000 years ago, and are up to 7 metres (23 feet) deep.

Ireland is also famously boggy, and no doubt its rural whiskey makers burned peat, but distilling quickly moved to an industrial scale, concentrated in the few big cities, and the lack of peat became a defining characteristic of the "smooth" Irish whiskies. The large, urban distillers used coke to fire smokeless maltings. Having been overtaken in volume long ago by the country next door, the Irish are now rediscovering the merit of variety. A peated single malt called Connemara was launched in 1995–96 by the Cooley distillery, and has gone on to win several judgings.

HEATHER

In the unofficial national anthem, the "Flower of Scotland" is Robert the Bruce; in heraldry, it is the thistle; in the world of drinks, it is surely heather. While the thistle is Scotland (prickly, defensive, and looking for a fight), heather is attractive and lucky. In Scotland, especially Orkney, it was traditionally the flavouring for an ale. When a whisky has a floral aroma, the flower is frequently heather. Often, it is not the flower itself but heather honey.

The colour purple
Heather is a distinctive feature of the Scottish landscape. Its colour does not affect the whisky, but the floral and honey aromas often seem to have jumped into the glass.

These characteristics are especially notable on Speyside and Aberdeenshire, where the hills are dense with heather. Glen Elgin and Balvenie are two whiskies with a notably heather-honey character. In Aberdeenshire, Glendronach and Glen Garioch have an enjoyable touch of heather, balancing their dry maltiness.

Heather is a significant component of much peat in Scotland. At some distilleries, notably Highland Park, lore has it that sprigs of heather were thrown on to the peat fire in the maltings. Water flows over heather to several distilleries. Besoms, or brooms, made of heather twigs were once commonplace in Scotland, and were typically used to clean wooden washbacks (fermenting vessels). Whether their effect was to sanitize or inadvertently to inoculate with micro-organisms is a piquant question. Wild yeast activity is at its height in summer, when bees are pollinating, and heather is a favourite source of nectar.

The Greek for the word "brush" gives us the botanical name *Calluna vulgaris* for the purple ling heather, which carpets the hillsides from mid-August into September. The brighter, redder bell heather (*Erica cinerea*) and the pinker, cross-leafed variety (*Erica tetralix*) flower about a month earlier. The English name for this group of small evergreen shrubs derives from their liking of heaths, but they also grow in bogs and on mountainsides. All three occur in Scotland, where heather covers between 1.6 and 2 million hectares (4 to 5 million acres).

Some varieties are found throughout northern Europe, others are native to Scotland, which has the greatest abundance of the plants. Scottish settlers introduced heather to North America.

BARLEY

Everyone knows that wines and brandies are made from grapes, but what about beer or whisky? Many consumers are unsure. Beer is often thought, mistakenly, to be made from hops. And whisky?

In explaining, and therefore promoting, its natural qualities, the grape does rather better than the grain. Wine makers often indicate on their labels which varieties of grape they have used. They may do this even if the wine is not a varietal. They might even discuss their choice of grape varieties on a back label or hang tag, and in their public relations and advertising.

Whisky makers do not in general do this. Why not? Are they using poor-quality barley? No. Malting requires barley of good quality. The argument for reticence is threefold: barley's contribution to flavour in whisky is less than it would be in beer, and even less than that of the grapes in wine. Second, perhaps simply as a reflection of the above,

The grapes of Scotch
In the familiar, alliterative phrase "the grape and the grain", the first ingredient is better understood than the second. These grains of malted barley will become whisky.

the difference between varieties is less obvious when it comes to flavour. Third, perhaps explaining this, the act of distillation removes some characteristics, and others are masked by the flavours gained during maturation. All of this is true up to a point, but what the distiller puts into his vessels must be a factor in the liquid that issues from them.

Almost all whisky distillers buy their barley according to a set of technical criteria (corn size, nitrogen, moisture content, etc.), rather than by variety. Some varieties bred or selected in the period of innovation after the Second World War are still legends. The last of that line, Golden Promise, represented 95 per cent of the harvest at its peak. Its short straw stands up to the wind; it ripens early (in August); and it produces nutty, rich flavours.

As the industry has grown, farmers have switched to varieties that give them more grain per acre, and therefore increase their profitability, while distillers have sought varieties that yield more fermentable sugars. These, however, do not necessarily produce delicious flavours, any more than do bigger, redder strawberries out of season. Nor do the varieties last much more than four or five seasons before being overtaken by something "better".

SEAWEED

The medicinal note in most Islay malts, especially Laphroaig, surely derives from seaweed, a source of iodine. The sea washes against the walls at all the distilleries, except Bruichladdich, and the coast is enwrapped with seaweed. How do the seaweedy, iron-like aromas get into the spirit? It seems likely that they are carried ashore by the winds and the rain, and permeate the peaty surface of the island. Then, when the rivers and burns flow over the peat to the distilleries, they pick up these flavours and impart them in the steep or the mash tun. If the boggy surface is, indeed, impregnated with the seaweedy rain, then a further opportunity will arise when the peat is cut and burned in the distillery's maltings.

The greatest scepticism concerns the belief that the casks in the warehouses "breathe in" the atmosphere. Distillers who use centralized warehouses, away from the distillery, especially favour this argument. Some age on site spirit which is destined to be bottled as single malt, but send to centralized warehouses spirit that is destined for blending.

Seaweed has been described as one of Scotland's most abundant natural resources. The harvesting of seaweed was once a significant industry in Scotland. There is some circumstantial evidence that the practice was introduced by monks on the islands of the west. This is the part of Scotland with the most seaweed. Skye has especially dense kelp forests, sometimes stretching 5 kilometres (3 miles) offshore and more than 20 metres (65 feet) deep. In the islands, kelp was traditionally used as a fertilizer. It was also collected as a source of iodine. More recently, it was used to provide alginates to clarify beer and set jellies and desserts.

Lagavulin's lordly terroir
Where the Lords of the Isles defended their territory, the land and seascape have an elemental appearance. There is seaweed on the rocks and Port Ellen's peat smoke in the air.

The infusion
Like coffee in a filter, the ground grains of malted barley are soaked in warm water, in a vessel with a sieve-like base. The stirring mechanism rotates and can be lowered so that its blades prevent the mixture from solidifying.

FLAVOURS SHAPED AT THE DISTILLERY

In the balance of influences, much more importance has been accorded in recent years to the way in which the distillery works. Twenty-seven malt distilleries, (about a third of the industry's working total) are owned by Diageo, the world's biggest drinks group; and Diageo argues strongly that the most important influences on flavour come from within the distillery itself.

The basic process of making malt whisky is the same throughout Scotland, but there are endless small but significant areas of variation. The degree of peating in the malt is one, similar to the choice of roasts in coffee. Another example is the density (or original gravity) of the malt-and-water mixture that goes into the mash tun (the "coffee filter"). The time the mixture spends in the mash tun, the temperatures to which it is raised, and the duration of each stage, all vary slightly from one distillery to the next. Inside a traditional mash tun is a system of revolving rakes to stir the mixture. In the more modern lauter system, developed in the German brewing industry, a system of knives is used. The German word "lauter" means pure or transparent, and refers to the solution of malt sugars that emerges from the vessel.

As in cooking, every variation affects everything that follows, so that the permutations are infinite. It can be very difficult to determine which aspect of procedure has what effect. Despite that, the industry in general has over the years adopted a rather casual attitude towards yeast's use in fermentation. The view taken was that yeast's influence on flavour would largely be lost in distillation, and that its job was simply to produce as much alcohol as possible.

For years, almost all of Scotland's malt distillers employed the same two yeast cultures. An ale yeast from one of the big brewers was used because it started quickly. Then there was a second pitching with a whisky yeast from Distillers' Company Limited (now long subsumed into a component of Diageo). This had less speed but more staying power. Mergers and changes in ownership resulted in different yeasts coming into the industry. Many distilleries now use only one culture; even Macallan, who insisted on three, have retreated to two.

The action of yeast in fermentation creates flavour compounds called "esters", which are variously fruity, nutty, and spicy. It is difficult to accept that none of these would survive distillation. Diageo believes that the amount of time spent in the fermenter is critical to the individuality of each distillate. The effect of a new yeast culture can be tasted in new make, but the final result will not be determined until the whisky is mature.

Fermentation vessels in Scottish malt distilleries are known as "washbacks". Some are closed vessels made of metal, usually stainless steel. These are easy to clean and relatively safe from contaminants. Despite this, some distilleries prefer wooden washbacks, usually made from larch or Oregon pine. These are open, with a movable lid. Although they are cleaned thoroughly, it is hard to believe that they accommodate no resident microflora. Perhaps these contribute to the house character of some of the more interesting whiskies. Meanwhile, whether the microclimate in and around the distillery has an influence is hotly debated.

Anyone who cooks will know that a recipe, however rigidly followed, will produce different results every time, depending upon the source of heat, the utensils, the cook, and so forth. The design of the stills is a factor increasingly emphasized by Diageo, but even this has an element of location. Some farmhouse distilleries clearly had stills designed to fit their limited space. Elsewhere, several distilleries in the same valley will have the same shape of still (in much the same way that railway stations on the same line may look alike). Obviously, the local coppersmith had his own way of doing things. Distilleries are reluctant to change the shape or size of their stills when wear and tear demands replacement, or when an expansion is planned. The

Water music?
Not a French horn, or any musical instrument, but the unromantically named worm tub. This one, at a smaller distillery, has a 24.5 metre (80 ft) "worm". This technique produces richer whiskies than more modern methods.

legend is that if a worn-out still has been dented at some time, the coppersmith will beat a similar blemish into its replacement, in order to ensure that the same whisky emerges.

Illegal distillers used just one small (and therefore portable), copper pot. Since then stills have grown, and are typically run in pairs (or occasionally threesomes), but the principles have not changed. It is clear that design has been largely empirical, with experiments and innovations introduced by individuals. It is often hard to imagine how a bit of extra piping here or there can make a difference. The ratio of surface areas to heat, liquid, vapour, and condensate have infinite effects that are not fully understood.

It is argued that in a tall, narrow still, much of the vapour will condense before it can escape. The condensate will fall back into the still and be redistilled. This is known as reflux. The result is a more thorough distillation and a more delicate spirit. Because there is far less reflux in a short, fat still, the spirit will be oilier, creamier, and richer. This is just the simplest example of the shape influencing the character of the whisky.

Stills vary enormously in size and shapes range from "lantern" or "lamp" to "onion" or "pear". Some have a mini-column above the shoulders or, more often, a "boil ball". Others have pipes known as "purifiers" in order to create reflux. The pipe that carries the vapour to the condenser is sometimes at an upward angle, or it can be straight, or point downward. The first will create the most reflux and the last little or none.

The traditional method of condensing is in a worm tub. The vapours pass through a worm-like coil of copper piping in a tub of cold water. This tends to produce a more pungent, characterful spirit, with a heavier, maltier, cereal-grain character.

The more modern system has the opposite relationship between vapour and water. It involves a single large tube, inside which are packed smaller tubes. The small tubes are circulated with cold water,

Still life
The stills at Talisker Distillery. In 1960, a lapse in concentration led to an overflow of the then coal-fired still. The resultant fire burnt down the distillery, which was subsequently rebuilt as an exact copy.

while the vapour passes through the large tube. This is called a shell-and-tube condenser. It is more efficient, and is said to produce lighter, grassier, fruitier spirits.

At a time when the industry was moving from worm tubs to shell-and-tube, Diageo made this change at its Dalwhinnie distillery. It was subsequently decided that the spirit had changed character to an unacceptable degree, and the distillery reverted to worm tubs.

One of the most important judgments in influencing flavour is deciding the speed at which the stills are run. Equally important is the decision about when the process has arrived at an acceptable spirit.

In maturation, most distillery managers prefer a stone-built, earth-floored, cool, damp warehouse. Such an atmosphere is felt to encourage the casks to breathe. In this type of structure, known as a dunnage warehouse, the casks are normally stacked only three high, usually with planks between them as supports. The more modern type of warehouse has a concrete floor and fixed racking. As is often the case, the old, inefficient system, more vulnerable to the vagaries of nature, produces the more characterful result.

REGIONAL VARIATIONS

LIKE WINES – AND MANY OTHER DRINKS – the single malts of Scotland usually identify in their labelling not only their country of origin but also the region within it. To know where in Scotland a whisky was produced is to have a very general idea of its likely character. The differences arise from *terroir* and tradition; there are no regional regulations regarding production methods. In their aroma and palate, some whiskies speak of their region more clearly than others, as is the case with wines. Within Bordeaux, a particular Pomerol, for example, might have a richness more reminiscent of Burgundy; similar comparisons can be made in Scotland.

THE LOWLANDS

These are the most accessible whiskies, in both palate and geography, but sadly few in number. From the border town of Carlisle, it is less than 160 kilometres (100 miles) to the southernmost Scottish distillery, Bladnoch, which has been back in production since December 2000, albeit on a limited scale. It is distilling twice a week for half the year. Spirit tasted at 18 months as work in progress was malty, oily, dry, and very flowery. Mature whisky is not expected until 2008–10. Meanwhile, in the shop, distillery rescuer Raymond Armstrong offers a Flora and Fauna edition of Bladnoch, and various independent bottlings produced by former owners Diageo/UDV.

Only two Lowlanders are in constant production. One of these is Auchentoshan, sometimes billed as "Glasgow's only working distillery". It is on the edge of the city, at Dalmuir, across the Dunbartonshire county line. In Lowland tradition, the whisky is light in both flavour and body, but surprisingly complex and herbal. Auchentoshan is now the sole practitioner of the Lowland tradition of triple distillation. The distillery does not have a visitor centre, but professional tours are possible by arrangement. With its galleried mash house and uncluttered still-house, it is very visitor-friendly.

Maritime malt
Rivetted, not welded, this pot still has a marine appearance befitting its region. Campbeltown's heyday was the era of coastal steamers. Fat stills make oily, muscular whiskies.

The other thriving Lowlander, at the opposite side of the country, is Glenkinchie, "The Edinburgh Malt". This pretty distillery is about 25 kilometres (15 miles) southeast of the city, in the direction of the border. Its spicy whisky has a popular following, and the distillery has a visitor centre.

There were never a great many Lowland malts, but to have only three active distilleries is perilously few. The delicacy of the Lowlanders makes its own contribution to the world of single malts. This style can be very attractive, especially to people who find the Highlanders and Islanders too robust.

The Lowlanders' problem has been that the Highlanders and Islanders have the romance. Many consumers like a gentle, sweetish malt such as is typical in the Lowlands, but they want the label to say it came from the Highlands. This is analogous with the wine industry, where consumers who like sweetish Chardonnays nevertheless insist that they are drinking a "dry white".

The notion of the Lowlands as a whisky region would be reinforced if it could annex two distilleries that are barely across the Highland line: Glengoyne and Loch Lomond. The first is very pretty, can be visited, and is barely outside Glasgow. Its malty whisky would be perfectly acceptable as a Lowlander. The second is a more industrial site, but a much more attractive distillery than it once was, and it makes a variety of whiskies. Pressed to "defect", both would probably cling to the Highland designation.

THE HIGHLANDS

The border between the Lowland and Highland distilleries is surprisingly southerly, following old county boundaries, stretching across the country between the rivers Clyde and Tay. Some commentators talk of a "southern Highlands", embracing Tullibardine and Deanston. Beyond these two, the spread is clearly eastern.

SPEYSIDE is not precisely defined, but it embraces between a half and two-thirds of Scotland's distilleries, including the most widely recognized whisky names. A generous definition of Speyside is assumed in this book. Strictly speaking, the long-gone distilleries of Inverness were regarded as Highlanders, not Speysiders. The same might be argued of Aberdeenshire distilleries like Glendronach, but it is easier for the visitor to regard this stretch of the Highlands as a contiguous region.

Highest and lowest
Its pagodas reaching for the clouds, Dalwhinnie, at 327 metres (1,073 ft), is one of the highest distilleries, with the lowest average temperature. It also serves as a weather station for the meteorological office of the United Kingdom.

Again for the convenience of the visitor, this book divides the region into a series of river valleys. In some of these valleys, there do seem to be similarities between the whiskies of neighbouring distilleries.

The River Spey itself is lined with distilleries on both banks, but a number of tributaries and adjoining rivers frame the region. Speyside's ascendancy rested not only on the Grampian mountain snow-melt and the malting barley of Banff and Moray, but also on the railway era. Trains on a rustic branch alongside the Spey took workers and barley or malt to the distilleries, and returned with whisky for the main line to Edinburgh, Glasgow, and London. Only vestiges of the Speyside railway survive today, though it is a popular walk. The active line from Aberdeen to Inverness (just over 160 kilometres or 100 miles) follows the main road. The rivers are crossed as follows:

DEVERON: This valley has Glendronach distillery and Glen Deveron. There are five or six distilleries in the general area, but these are quite widely dispersed. Most produce firm, malty whiskies.

ISLA: This has nothing to do with island (it has a different spelling; there's no "y"). Dominican monks brewed here in the 1200s, and there is mention of heather ale in the records. The oldest distillery on

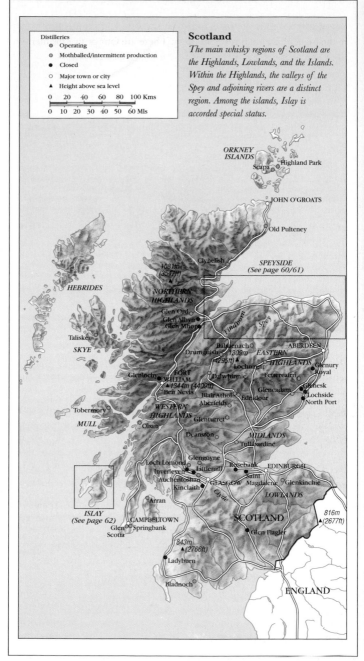

Distilleries
- ◉ Operating
- ◉ Mothballed/intermittent production
- ● Closed
- ○ Major town or city
- ▲ Height above sea level

0   20   40   60   80   100 Kms
0   10   20   30   40   50   60 Mls

Scotland

The main whisky regions of Scotland are the Highlands, Lowlands, and the Islands. Within the Highlands, the valleys of the Spey and adjoining rivers are a distinct region. Among the islands, Islay is accorded special status.

ORKNEY
ISLANDS
Scapa ● Highland Park

JOHN O'GROATS

Old Pulteney

Clynelish

108m
(3547ft)
▲

SPEYSIDE
(See page 60/61)

HEBRIDES

NORTHERN
HIGHLANDS

Glen Ord
Glen Albyn
Glen Mhor

Findhorn   Spey

Talisker

ABERDEEN

SKYE

Balmenach

Drumguish ▲*1309m*
(4295ft) Lochnagar
Dalwhinnie

EASTERN
HIGHLANDS

Glenury
Royal

Glenlochy

FORT
WILLIAM
▲*1344m (4409ft)*
Ben Nevis

Fettercairn
Glencadam   Glenesk
Lochside
North Port

Blair Athol
Edradour
Aberfeldy

WESTERN
HIGHLANDS

Tobermory

Glenturret

MULL

Oban

Deanston

MIDLANDS
Tullibardine

ISLAY
(See page 62)

Loch Lomond
Glengoyne
Inverleven Littlemill
Auchentoshan
Kinclaith

Rosebank
EDINBURGH
Saint
Magdalene Glenkinchie

LOWLANDS

GLASGOW

Clyde

816m
▲*(2677ft)*

CAMPBELTOWN
Glen Springbank
Scotia

Arran

SCOTLAND

Glen Flagler

843m
▲*(2766ft)*

Ladyburn

Bladnoch

ENGLAND

36

Speyside is Strathisla (founded in 1786), showpiece of Chivas Brothers, in the town of Keith in the Isla Valley. There are four or five distilleries in this area, and some of its whiskies have a cedary dryness.

FIDDICH AND DULLAN: These rivers meet at Dufftown, one of the claimants to be the whisky capital of Scotland. There are still six working distilleries in the area, despite the loss of Pittyvaich in 2002. A couple more are currently silent. Some classically rounded, malty Speysiders are produced here, including the secret star, Mortlach.

LIVET: The most famous distillery is called after the river valley itself, and there are three others in the area, all producing light, soft, delicate whiskies. The Livet appellation was once widely copied, but has been increasingly protected. The hill town, Tomintoul, is a base for exploration.

SPEY: The most whiskied stretch of the river flows from the pretty Craggannmore distillery (producing a complex malt), via Knockando and Cardhu (lighter and more flowery), Macallan and Aberlour (malty and often sherryish) to the village of Craigellachie, a good base from which to explore.

ROTHES BURN: Actually no more than a stream, this river is one of several that reach the Spey at Rothes, another whisky "capital". This

Restless river
Highland backdrop of rock, conifers, heather, and scorched earth. The mountains send the fast-flowing river Spey toward the distilleries that it baptises.

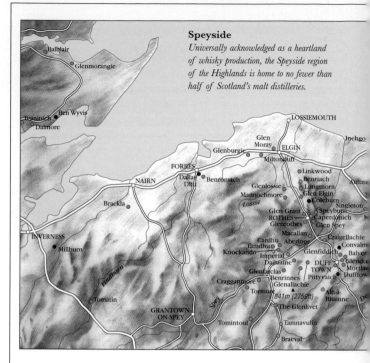

Speyside

Universally acknowledged as a heartland of whisky production, the Speyside region of the Highlands is home to no fewer than half of Scotland's malt distilleries.

one-street town has five distilleries, producing some very nutty whiskies. Speyburn, usually shot through the trees, is the most photographed distillery in Scotland, while Glen Grant has a spectacular "tropical" garden, a coppersmith's, and a "dark grains" plant, which turns residual malt into cattle feed.

LOSSIE: Was it the water that first attracted the Benedictines of Pluscarden to this region? They no longer brew there, but they still have a priory next door to the Miltonduff distillery. Two secret stars, Longmorn and Linkwood, are among the eight distilleries just south of Elgin. The world's most famous whisky shop, Gordon & MacPhail, is in Elgin itself. This sometimes ornate Victorian town is the undisputed commercial capital of Speyside and the county seat of Moray. The Lossie whiskies are sweetish and malty.

FINDHORN: Born-again Benromach is near the town Forres. Production restarted in 1998: the new make tasted creamy and flowery. The museum distillery of Dallas Dhu is nearby, and in the distance is Tomatin.

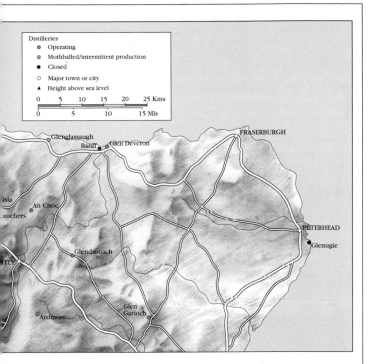

Distilleries
- ◉ Operating
- ◉ Mothballed/intermittent production
- ● Closed
- ○ Major town or city
- ▲ Height above sea level

0   5   10   15   20   25 Kms
0   5   10   15 Mls

Glenglassaugh
Banff   Glen Deveron
FRASERBURGH
isla
An Cnoc
auchers
PETERHEAD
Glenugie
Glendronach
TLY
Glen
Garioch
Ardmore

THE NORTHERN HIGHLANDS is a geographically clear-cut region, which runs from Inverness, straight up the last stretch of the east coast. The region's water commonly runs over sandstone, and there is a gentle maritime influence. There are four or five distilleries in short order; including the smooth Glen Ord, the energetic Glenmorangie and the rich Dalmore. Then there is a gap before the connoisseurs' favourite, Clynelish, and an even bigger gap before the famously salty Old Pulteney in Wick. As its distilleries have become more active, the northern Highlands has gained more recognition as a region. Its whiskies tend toward firm, crisp dryness and a light saltiness.

WESTERN HIGHLANDS The far northwest is the only sizeable stretch of the country with no legal whisky makers. It is just too rugged and rocky. Even the centre cut has only two distilleries. On the foothills of Scotland's (and Britain's) highest mountain, Ben Nevis, the eponymous distillery can be regarded as being "coastal", according to its manager, Colin Ross. Why? Because it is on a sea loch. The Oban distillery certainly does face the sea, and has the flavours to prove it.

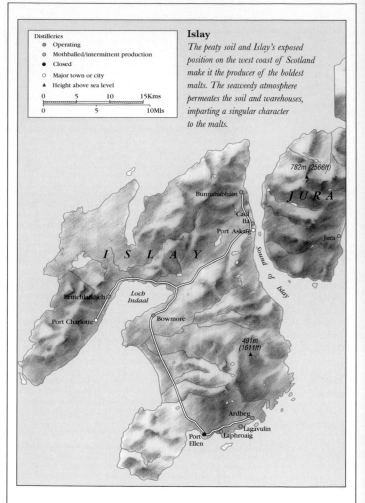

Distilleries
- ◉ Operating
- ◎ Mothballed/intermittent production
- ● Closed
- ○ Major town or city
- ▲ Height above sea level

| 0 | 5 | 10 | 15Kms |
| 0 | | 5 | 10Mls |

Islay

The peaty soil and Islay's exposed position on the west coast of Scotland make it the producer of the boldest malts. The seaweedy atmosphere permeates the soil and warehouses, imparting a singular character to the malts.

782m (2566ft)

J U R A

Bunnahabhain

Caol Ila

Port Askaig

Jura

I S L A Y

Sound of Islay

Bruichladdich

Loch Indaal

Port Charlotte

Bowmore

491m (1611ft) ▲

Ardbeg

Lagavulin

Port Ellen

Laphroaig

THE ISLANDS

The greatest whisky island by far is Islay (above), with its eight distilleries, all of which are operating. The others have one apiece, except for Orkney, which has two distilleries.

ORKNEY For the moment, Highland Park is Scotland's northernmost distillery. Its whisky is one of the greats, peaty and smoky, but a superb all-rounder. Saltier whiskies from the Scapa distillery have a strong following, but are not in production at the moment.

Determined distillery
It looks neat and secure, but the Talisker Distillery determinedly clings to a steep hillside, which drops down to a seaweedy loch. Its location is remote, even within the somewhat lunar Isle of Skye.

SHETLAND The first ever legal distillery in Shetland was planned for 2004, but is still seeking investors – it will be Scotland's most northerly.

SKYE Skye's only whisky is the classic Talisker – volcanic, explosive, and peppery. The taste reflects the wild, looming *terroir*.

MULL Tobermory is a restrained islander, but the distillery also produces the peatier, smokier Ledaig. It is to be hoped that Tobermory does not suffer from its parent's acquisition of Bunnahabhain.

JURA The decidedly piney Isle of Jura whisky has appeared in more expressions and has been better promoted since the owning group, Whyte and Mackay, seceded from its American parent, Jim Beam.

ISLAY The Islay Festival in late May is increasingly popular. Long established distilleries like Caol Ila are making their malts much more available as singles; other distilleries have emerged from mothballs.

ARRAN The newest distillery in Scotland, Arran ran its first spirit in 1995. Its small stills produce a creamy spirit with only faint touches of island character: a touch of flowery pine in the finish.

WHEN A MALT IS BLENDED

THE GREEN REVOLUTION

The word "malt" is confusingly versatile. To malt grain is to steep it in water and dry it in a kiln with a view to rendering it soluble. The premier grain from which Scotch whisky is produced is barley. After being steeped and kilned, this is variously described as malted barley. Or barley malt. Or simply malt. I sometimes wonder whether my adult taste in drinks was planted by the dark malt syrup I was given as a tonic when I was a boy. Or the malt-flavoured milk shakes that the prettiest girls drank at the soda fountain in American movies. There is something both wholesome and sexy about the word. Lovers of malt whisky often use the term as an abbreviation for the drink, as in "an Islay malt" or "a Highland malt".

MALT WHISKY is a term indicating a whisky made entirely from malted barley, in a batch process, in a traditional pot still. This type of still resembles a copper cooking pot or kettle. Shapes of pot stills vary, and are a significant influence on flavour. Malt Whisky, and sometimes Pure Malt Whisky, are general terms. They do not specify whether a whisky is a Single Malt or a Blended Malt (see below).

SINGLE MALT WHISKY is defined as above, with the essential proviso that all the whisky in the bottle was produced in one distillery. Whiskies from more than 100 malt distilleries (about three quarters of them working at any one time) are available. The whiskies of each distillery have their own house character, with further variations according to age, strength and style of maturation. This individuality of character, and the overall diversity it represents, has increasingly been explored in recent years. If the consumer particularly enjoys the whisky of the Caol Ila distillery, for example, or wishes to try Talisker, the phrase Single Malt on the label means that the bottle contains nothing else.

Perfecting the blend
Dr. Jim Beveridge, the Johnnie Walker Master Blender, noses Cardhu malt whisky at the Cardhu distillery – also known as the home of Johnnie Walker.

BLENDED MALT WHISKY. This is a blend of malt whiskies from different distilleries. If a Single Malt is a soloist, a Blended Malt Whisky might be a small group of virtuoso musicians playing together: distinctive voices but in harmony, suggest Johnnie Walker, in discussing their Green Label Blended Malt Scotch Whisky. The increasing consumer interest in malts has led to the creation of such combinations as a further exposition of the whisky-maker's art. A product like Green Label also offers devotees of Johnnie Walker a malt within their own favoured range. Green Label is the most visible among whiskies identified as Blended Malts. This term was introduced in 2005 by the industry's trade body, the Scotch Whisky Association. Previously, this style was simply labelled as Malt Whisky, Pure Malt, or by the industry term Vatted Malt, which was thought to be confusing to some consumers. An alternative worry is that the term Blended Malt risks confusing two categories, and blurring the special identity of malt whisky. Green Label contains malts from the islands of Islay and Skye, and from Speyside. It is clearly intended to have that lively, virtuoso character. Some Blended Malts are designed to highlight the characteristics of a single region; others to create an "own brand" for a restaurant or shop; yet others perhaps provide a stepping stone to single malts.

BLENDED SCOTCH WHISKY. The art of blending whisky developed in the mid 1800s, around the time when John Walker was building his retail business in Kilmarnock, Scotland. Retailers like the Walker family made their own blends in order to offer viable volumes of consistent whisky. Distilling is an agricultural industry, subject to harvests and weather. The malt distilleries in the glens of the Grampian mountains, the valley of the Spey and the Scottish islands, continued to impart character to the Blended Scotch Whisky made by Johnnie Walker long after its blends were leavened with lighter whiskies made from other grains (for example unmalted barley, wheat or maize) in column-shaped continuous stills. Today, Blended Scotch Whisky implies a substantial proportion of grain whisky (typically more than half). Critics argue that the natural dynamic of blending is toward a common denominator, making for whiskies that are similar. Over the years, Johnnie Walker has added more blends. They are clearly a family, but each has its own character: Red, Black, Gold and Blue are all Blended Scotches. Green is a Blended Malt.

Still going strong ... and still innovating.

JOHNNIE WALKER GREEN LABEL

PRODUCER Diageo
WEBSITE www.johnniewalker.com

T HE MOST WIDELY KNOWN NAME in Scotch whisky began with a farming family in the Lowland county of Ayrshire. The Walkers invested in a provision merchant and wine and spirit shop in the town of Kilmarnock in 1820. The founder's grandson, Alexander Walker, created Red Label in 1909, and it became the world's best-selling blended Scotch whisky. Over the years, there have been nine or ten variations on the theme, most identified by the colour of the famously slanted label, on the distinctive oblong bottle. All of these were Blended Scotch Whiskies until the launch of Green Label, initially in France, in 1996. This was originally described as Pure Malt. It was launched internationally in 2000, and has since 2005 been identified as a Blended Malt Whisky. In the course of its history, Johnnie Walker has owned several malt distilleries, most famously Cardhu and Talisker. The company is one of the principal components of Diageo.

HOUSE STYLE Big, muscular, but smooth. With Chinese food? Hunan or Szechuan.

JOHNNIE WALKER GREEN LABEL, 15-year-old, 43 vol

COLOUR	Not-quite ripe tangerine.
NOSE	Pralines. Lemon skins. Almonds.
BODY	Oily, creamy.
PALATE	Spicy. Cinnamon. Ginger cake.
FINISH	Drying. Flapjack. Gunpowder tea. Pepper. Salt.

SCORE **82**

A–Z
OF SINGLE MALTS

WHATEVER THE ARGUMENTS about their relative prices, no one denies that a Château Latour is more complex than a mass-market table wine. The fine wines of the whisky world are the single malts. Some malts are made to higher standards than others, and some are inherently more distinctive than their neighbours. This cannot be obscured by the producers' blustery arguments about "personal taste". A tasting note cannot be definitive, but it can be a useful guide, and will tell you, for example, if the whisky is a light, dry malt, or if it is rich and sherryish, or peaty and smoky.

The tasting notes start with a comment on the house style – a quick, first, general indication of what to expect from each distillery's products, before looking at the variations that emerge in different ages and bottlings. I also suggest the best moment for each distillery's whiskies (such as before dinner, or with a book at bedtime). These suggestions are meant as an encouragement to try each in a congenial situation. They are not meant to be taken with excessive seriousness.

Tasting note example:

AUCHENTOSHAN 1973, 29-year-old, Sherry Butt No 793, 55.8 vol

COLOUR Pinkish red. Almost rhubarb-like.
NOSE Jammy. Australian Shiraz. Red apples. Peaches.
BODY Textured. Fluffy.
PALATE An extraordinarily fruity whisky, with peach dominant. Peach-stone flavours, too. Underneath all that, it is hard to divine any Auchentoshan character. Severely marked down for those reasons.
FINISH Nutty dryness. With the cheese? After dinner?

SCORE **69**

COLOUR The natural colour of a malt matured in plain wood is a very pale yellow. Darker shades, ranging from amber to ruby to deep brown, can be imparted by sherry wood. Some distilleries use casks

A character-forming home
Skye forms a natural crucible, in which the flavours of a great whisky are fused. Living in the mountains and surrounded by sea, the whisky assumes a gusty salt-and-pepper house character.

that have been treated with concentrated sherry, and this can cause a caramel-like appearance and palate. Some add caramel to balance the colour. I do not suggest that one colour is in itself better than another, though a particular subtle hue can heighten the pleasure of a fine malt. We enjoy food and drink with our eyes as well as our nose and palate.

NOSE Anyone sampling any food or drink experiences much of the flavour through the sense of smell. Whisky is highly aromatic, and the aromas of malts include peat, flowers, honey, toasty maltiness, coastal brine, and seaweed, for example.

BODY Lightness, smoothness, or richness might refresh, soothe, or satisfy. Body and texture (sometimes known as "mouth feel") are distinct features of each malt.

PALATE In the enjoyment of any complex drink, each sip will offer new aspects of the taste. Even one sip will gradually unfold a number of taste characteristics in different parts of the mouth over a period of, say, a minute. This is notably true of single malts. Some present a very extensive development of palate. A taster working with an unfamiliar malt may go back to it several times over a period of days, in search of its full character. I have adopted this technique in my tastings for this book.

FINISH In all types of alcoholic drink, the "finish" is a further stage of the pleasure. In most single malts, it is more than a simple aftertaste, however important that may be. It is a crescendo, followed by a series of echoes. When I leave the bottle, I like to be whistling the tune. When the music of the malt fades, there is recollection in tranquillity.

SCORE The pleasures described above cannot be measured with precision, if at all. The scoring system is intended merely as a guide to the status of the malts. Each tasting note is given a score out of 100. This is inspired by the system of scoring wines devised by the American writer Robert Parker. In this book, a rating in the 50s indicates a malt that in my view lacks balance or character, and which – in fairness – was probably never meant to be bottled as a single. The 60s suggest an enjoyable but unexceptional malt. Anything in the 70s is worth tasting, especially above 75. The 80s are, in my view, distinctive and exceptional. The 90s are the greats.

A modest score should not dissuade anyone from trying a malt. Perhaps I was less than enthusiastic; you might love it.

ABERLOUR

PRODUCER Chivas Brothers
REGION Highlands DISTRICT Speyside (Strathspey)
ADDRESS Aberlour, Banffshire, AB3 9PJ
TEL 01340 881249 WEBSITE www.aberlour.co.uk VC

Having acquired Chivas in 2002, with its dazzling family of Speyside distilleries (The Glenlivet, Glen Grant, and Longmorn are but three), will French parents Pernod Ricard still love Aberlour? It was their Number One son; now it has siblings. The whisky is well respected in Scotland, but its greatest popularity, based on merit as much as on adoptive parentage, is in France. At the Speyside Festival in May, the distillery has hosted a series of whisky dinners created by spirited writer Martine Nouet.

Aberlour is at least a super-middleweight in body. With medals galore in recent years, it competes as a light-heavyweight, standing up well against bigger names, much as Georges Carpentier did. Aberlour rhymes with "power" in English, but most French-speakers make it sound more like "amour".

The regular range in Scotland and the rest of the United Kingdom comprises the 10-year-old, the a'bunadh, and the 15-year-old sherry wood finish, but there are larger selections in duty-free and in France. The overall range includes a great many minor variations.

Since 2002, visitors to the distillery have been able to hand-fill their own personally labelled bottle of Aberlour, from an identified single cask. A sherry butt and a bourbon barrel, each felt to provide a good example of its style, are set aside for this purpose. As each is exhausted, it is replaced by a similar cask. This personalized whisky is bottled at cask strength.

On the main road (A95) that follows the eastern bank of the Spey, an 1890s lodge signals the distillery, which is hidden a couple of hundred yards into the glen of the river Lour (little more than a burn). The Lour flows into the Spey. The site was known for a well associated with St Drostan, from the epoch of St Columba. The distilling water is soft. It rises from the granite of Ben Rinnes, by way of a spring in the glen of the Allachie, and is piped half a mile to the distillery.

HOUSE STYLE Soft texture, medium to full flavours, nutty, spicy (nutmeg?), sherry-accented. With dessert, or after dinner, depending upon maturity.

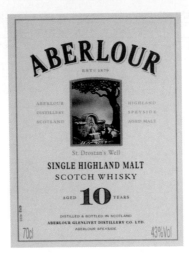

ABERLOUR 10-year-old, Principal Version, 43 vol

COLOUR Amber.

NOSE Malty, spicy, mint toffee.

BODY Remarkably soft and smooth. Medium to full.

PALATE Distinctively clinging mouth feel, with long-lasting flavour
development. Both sweetness and spicy, peppery dryness in its
malt character. Nutmeg and berry fruit.

FINISH Lingering, smooth, aromatic, clean.

SCORE 83

ABERLOUR a'bunadh ("The Origin"), No Age Statement, 59.6 vol

*A single malt comprising Aberlours from less than 10 to more than 15 years, vatted
together. All sherry-ageing, with an emphasis on second-fill dry oloroso. No chill filtration.
Mainly in duty-free and British Isles. In Victorian-style bottle.*

COLOUR Dark orange.

NOSE Sherry, mint, pralines. Luxurious, powerful.

BODY Full, creamy, textured, layered.

PALATE Rich, luxurious, and creamy, with a hint of
mint and cherries behind.

FINISH Nougat, cherry brandy, ginger, faint smoke.
Definitely after dinner.

SCORE 86

ABERLOUR a'bunadh Sterling Silver, 12-year-old, 58.7 vol

COLOUR Darker. Deep, shiny, chestnut.

NOSE Sherry, mint, pralines. Oakier and smokier than
the version above. Sherry. Black chocolate. Oil of peppermint.

BODY Big, firm.

PALATE Drier. Spicier. Ginger-and-plum preserve. More assertive.

FINISH Long. Lots of alcohol, but warming and soothing.
Prunes. Sappy, juicy fresh oak. Cedar. Cigar boxes.

SCORE 87

ABERLOUR 12-year-old, Sherry-matured, 43 vol

*Matured in first-fill dry oloroso. Originally marketed in France,
but now mainly found in duty-free.*

COLOUR Full amber.

NOSE Nutty, appetizing, relatively fresh, sherry aroma.

BODY Medium, soft.

PALATE Fresh, soft, malty. Soft liquorice, anis, hint of blackcurrant.

FINISH Silky, enwrapping, soothing.

SCORE 84

ABERLOUR 12-year-old, Double Cask Matured, 40 vol

Vatting of first-fill sherry and unspecified refill casks. Mainly for the French market.

COLOUR Bronze.

NOSE Earthy, fruity. Pears. Apples. Tarte tatin.

BODY Medium, firm.

PALATE Melty pastry. Caramel sauce. Custard (in this instance,
let's call it crème anglaise). Leaves of garden mint.

FINISH More of the mint. Now it has become spearmint.
Ends rather abruptly and sharply.

SCORE 82

ABERLOUR 16-year-old, Double Cask Matured, 43 vol

Same principle as the above. Also for the French market.

COLOUR Bronze red.

NOSE Seville oranges, lemons. Turkish delight. Rose-water.

BODY Gently rounded.

PALATE Smooth. Spun sugar. Caramel. Tightly combined flavours.
The extra years have made a big difference.

FINISH Cinnamon. Ground nutmeg. Nutty.

SCORE 84

ARDBEG

PRODUCER Glenmorangie plc
REGION Islay DISTRICT South Shore
ADDRESS Port Ellen, Islay, Argyll, PA42 7EA
TEL 01496 302244 WEBSITE www.ardbeg.com
EMAIL oldkiln@ardbeg.com VC

ALREADY ONE OF THE WORLD'S GREAT DISTILLERIES in the days when single malts were a secret, and revived at a cost of millions (whether euros or dollars), Ardbeg shines ever more brightly. Its reopening was one of the first signs of the Islay revival, of which it has become both a principal element and a beneficiary. Its owners' ambitions for the distillery are being rewarded. So is their faith in young manager Stuart Thomson and his wife Jackie.

Her knowledge and energy "front of house" have consolidated the distillery's popularity with visitors. When Ardbeg reopened, one of the former kilns was turned into a shop, also offering tea, coffee, a dram, and a clootie (dumpling). The Old Kiln is also used by local people: it now serves meals, and has been the western venue for writer Martine Nouet's whisky dinners.

Ardbeg aficionados still cling to the hope that the second kiln may one day return to use. The maltings were unusual in that there were no fans, causing the peat smoke to permeate very heavily. This is evident in very old bottlings. The peaty origins of the water are also a big influence in the whisky's earthy, tar-like flavours. Some lovers of Ardbeg believe that an apple-wood, lemon-skin fruitiness derives from a recirculatory system in the spirit still.

The distillery traces its history to 1794. The maltings last worked in 1976–77, though supplies of their malted barley were no doubt eked out a little longer. Ardbeg closed in the early 1980s, but towards the end of that decade began to work again, albeit very sporadically, using malt from Port Ellen. Whisky produced at that time, but released by the new owners, is less tar-like than the old Ardbeg. Such heavily peated whisky as was inherited has been used in some vattings. The distillery is currently buying an especially heavily peated malt, the impact of which will be seen in bottlings in the course of the next six or seven years.

HOUSE STYLE Earthy, very peaty, smoky, salty, robust. A bedtime malt.

ARDBEG 10-year-old, 46 vol

COLOUR Fino sherry.

NOSE Smoke, brine, iodine dryness.

BODY Only medium to full, but very firm. A young light-heavyweight, not musclebound by age. Pound-for-pound, the hardest hitter in the Ardbeg team, though without the power conferred by the old maltings.

PALATE Skips sweetly along at first, then becomes mean and moody. Bottlings a little variable.

FINISH Hefty, lots of iodine.

SCORE 85

ARDBEG 17-year-old, 40 vol

COLOUR Full, shimmering, greeny gold.

NOSE Assertive, briney, seaweedy, tar-like. Hint of sulphur.

BODY Medium, oily. Very firm.

PALATE Peppery but also sweet. Cereal grains, oil, gorse. Tightly combined flavours. More mature and rounded, but still robust. Very appetizing.

FINISH Oily. Lemon skins. Freshly ground white pepper.

SCORE 86

ARDBEG 21-year-old, 56.3 vol

Slightly more assertive than an Adelphi bottling reviewed in the fourth edition of this book.

COLOUR Deeper. More refractive and oily. Greeny gold.

NOSE Firm, but aromas more tightly combined. As though the brine and iodine-like seaweed had permeated a stretch of hard, compacted sand.

BODY Firm, unyielding.

PALATE Instant hit of flavours. The maritime character overlaying pepper, lemons, fresh limes, bananas. (After that bracing walk on the beach, an afternoon of snoozy luxury with fruits and pastries?)

FINISH After the snooze, a hot shower with coal-tar soap. That characteristic tar-like smokiness and phenol.

SCORE 87

THE BALVENIE

PRODUCER William Grant & Sons Ltd
REGION Highlands DISTRICT Speyside (Dufftown)
ADDRESS Dufftown, Banffshire, AB55 4BB
TEL 01340 820373 WEBSITE www.thebalvenie.com

As SEDUCTIVELY HONEYED AS A SPEYSIDER can be; ever more aristocratic, in recent years introducing vintages as though they were eligible offspring, The Balvenie is increasingly recognized far from her domain. Her tendency toward voluptuousness, and her ready charm, win friends easily. A dalliance by the sea resulted in the birth, in 2001, of The Balvenie Islay Cask. Fellow Speysiders resented the notion of a whisky from their elevated territory even contemplating the addition of "Islay" to its name. Meanwhile, Islanders complained that The Balvenie was merely courting popularity. There have been no more Islay Casks. It was a holiday romance.

She may be a notably rich spirit, but Bad Penny offers the easiest mnemonic for Balvenie's vowel sounds. The Balvenie distillery was built in 1892 by the Grant family, who had already established Glenfiddich in 1886. It is highly unusual for a distillery to remain in the same ownership throughout its history, but both Glenfiddich and Balvenie have done so, on their original sites, which adjoin one another. One became the world's biggest selling malt and the other the epitome of luxury, but both were established, thriftily, with second-hand stills. Balvenie's are more bulbous, and that feature no doubt contributes to the distinct character of the whisky. The distillery also has its own small floor maltings, using barley from the family farm.

In 1990, Grant's added to the site a third distillery, Kininvie. This also produces a creamy spirit, but Kininvie has not thus far been bottled as a single malt. Adjoining the site is the silent Convalmore distillery, acquired by Grant's in 1992 to augment warehousing capacity.

Grant's site is at Dufftown, where the rivers Fiddich and Dullan meet on their way to the Spey. The Balvenie distillery is near the castle of the same name, which dates at least from the 1200s. The castle was at one stage known as Mortlach and was at another stage occupied by the Duff family, and is now owned by the nation of Scotland.

HOUSE STYLE The most honeyish of malts, with a distinctively orangey note. Luxurious. After dinner. Ages well.

THE BALVENIE Founder's Reserve, 10-year-old, 40 vol

Matured in 90% American oak and 10% sherry.

COLOUR Bright gold.

NOSE Orange-honey perfume. Musky. Faint hint of peat.

BODY Medium.

PALATE Honeyed sweetness drying to lightly spicy notes. Very lively. Just a touch of sherry.

FINISH A tingly surge of flavours, with lingering, syrupy honey.

SCORE **85**

THE BALVENIE Double Wood, 12-year-old, 40 vol

First- and second-fill bourbon casks, then six to twelve months in sweet oloroso casks.

COLOUR Amber.

NOSE Sherry and orange skins.

BODY Medium, rich.

PALATE Beautifully combined mellow flavours: nutty, sweet, sherry, very orangey fruitiness, heather, cinnamon spiciness.

FINISH Long, tingling. Very warming.

SCORE **87**

THE BALVENIE Single Barrel, 15-year-old, 50.4 vol

All first-fill bourbon casks.

COLOUR Pale gold.

NOSE Assertive. Dry, fresh oak. Heather. Rooty. Coconut. Lemon pith.

BODY Firm.

PALATE Lively. Cedar. Orange skins, pineapple-like sweetness and acidity.

FINISH Very dry. Peppery alcohol.

SCORE **85**

BANFF

PRODUCER DCL
REGION Highlands   DISTRICT Speyside (Deveron)
SITE OF FORMER DISTILLERY Inverboyndie, on B9139, 1 mile west of Banff

T HE HOUSE OF COMMONS was once supplied with whisky from this distillery, near the adjoining towns of Banff and MacDuff. The two face each other across the Deveron, where the river flows into the Moray firth. The county of Banffshire once stretched from the Deveron to the Spey. This eastern flank of Speyside embraced half the region's distilleries. It has fewer today, but it is still barley country, its coastal strip linking the Laich of Moray with Aberdeenshire. The county became Banff and Buchan and is now subsumed into Aberdeenshire.

The distillery, dating from at least 1824, closed in 1983, leaving a substantial amount of stock. Its buildings have gradually been dismantled, though remains loom through the sea mist. They are in a field next to a graveyard. The spirits of Banff are restless judging from the profusion of independent bottlings.

HOUSE STYLE Fragrant. Lemon grass. Sweet. Restorative or after dinner.

BANFF 1980, 21-year-old, Cask No 2914, Signatory Vintage, 43 vol

COLOUR Vinho verde.

NOSE Light. Fresh. Grassy.

BODY Light, creamy, appetizingly dryish.

PALATE Grassy. Oaty. A suggestion of golden syrup.

FINISH Kendal mint cake.

COMMENT A pleasant, easily drinkable malt.
Showing few signs of age, good or bad.

SCORE 70

BENRINNES

PRODUCER Diageo
REGION Highlands DISTRICT Speyside
ADDRESS Aberlour, Banffshire, AB38 9WN
TEL Contact via Dailuaine 01340 872500

As a mountain, Ben Rinnes spreads itself to two words and is hard to miss; as a distillery and a whisky, Benrinnes compounds itself so neatly that it is too easily overlooked. It is no novice. Benrinnes may have been founded as early as the 1820s, and was largely rebuilt in the 1950s. The distillery had a long association with the Crawford blends. Its malt whisky did not have official bottling until 1991, in a Flora and Fauna edition. Benrinnes' system of partial triple distillation places it among the handful of quirky, individualistic distilleries in the Diageo group.

HOUSE STYLE Big, creamy, smoky, flavoursome, long.
Restorative or after dinner.

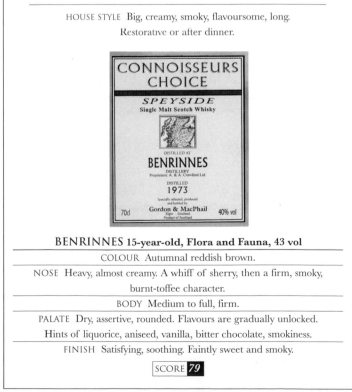

BENRINNES 15-year-old, Flora and Fauna, 43 vol

COLOUR Autumnal reddish brown.

NOSE Heavy, almost creamy. A whiff of sherry, then a firm, smoky, burnt-toffee character.

BODY Medium to full, firm.

PALATE Dry, assertive, rounded. Flavours are gradually unlocked. Hints of liquorice, aniseed, vanilla, bitter chocolate, smokiness.

FINISH Satisfying, soothing. Faintly sweet and smoky.

SCORE 79

BLAIR ATHOL

PRODUCER Diageo
REGION Highlands DISTRICT Eastern Highlands
ADDRESS Pitlochry, Perthshire, PH16 5LY
TEL 01796 482003
WEBSITE www.discovering-distilleries.com/www.malts.com VC

BLAIR IS A SCOTTISH NAME, referring to a tract of flat land, a clearance, a battlefield, or someone who originates from such a place. Blair Castle is the home of the Duke of Atholl. The village of Blair Atholl ends with a double "l", while the distillery prefers to keep it single. The distillery is nearby at the inland resort of Pitlochry, known for its summer theatre. The well-designed, beautifully maintained distillery, overgrown with ivy and Virginia creeper, traces its origins to 1798. It has been sympathetically expanded several times.

Its malt whisky is extensively used in the Bell's blends. The whisky matures quickly, and behaves like a gentleman. It is a sturdy, well-proportioned whisky rather than a big bruiser, but it can take a lot of sherry without becoming showy or belligerent.

HOUSE STYLE Redolent of shortbread and ginger cake. Spicy, nutty.
A mid-afternoon malt?

BLAIR ATHOL 12-year-old, 43 vol
*Released in 2000 in the Single Distillery Malt series, a further
development of the flora and fauna selections.*

COLOUR Attractive dark orange. Satin sheen.

NOSE Rich. Moist, cake-like. Lemon grass. Assam tea. (A hint of peat?)

BODY Silky smooth.

PALATE Spiced cake. Candied lemon-peels. Lots of flavour development.

FINISH Lightly smoky. Rooty. Treacley. Impeccable
balance between sweetness and dryness.

SCORE **78**

BLAIR ATHOL 12-year-old, Commemorative Limited Edition, 43 vol
A much more sherryish version.

COLOUR Distinctively deep. Orange liqueur.

NOSE Very complex. Fragrant, candied orange peels, dried fruit, cinnamon.

BODY Medium, silky.

PALATE Walnuts. Sweetish. Cakey. Faint treacle or molasses.

FINISH Very smooth, round, soothing, lightly smoky.
Very sophisticated for its age. Blair Athol matures quickly,
gaining perfuminess, sweetness, richness, spiciness, complexity,
and length. The sherry helps to emulsify the elements.

SCORE **77**

BLAIR ATHOL 18-year-old, Bicentenary Limited Edition, 56.7 vol

COLOUR Full peachy amber (but less dark than the 12-year-old).

NOSE Very delicate, finessed, orange and cinnamon.

BODY Bigger and firm.

PALATE Dates. Raisins. Dried figs. Moist cake. Butter.

FINISH Toasty. The slightly burnt crust on a cake.

SCORE **78**

BLAIR ATHOL 1981, Bottled 1997,
Cask Strength Limited Bottling, 55.5 vol
Now becoming hard to find.

COLOUR Deep, bright orange red.

NOSE Oakier and smokier, but appetizingly so.

BODY Medium, firm, smooth.

PALATE Delicious, clean toffee. Firm, slightly chewy. Pronounced black
treacle. Lively. Hints of banana, orange, lemon. Faint fragrant smokiness.

FINISH Ginger, toasty oak.

SCORE **78**

BOWMORE

PRODUCER Morrison Bowmore Distillers Ltd
REGION Islay DISTRICT Lochindaal
ADDRESS Bowmore, Islay, Argyll, PA34 7JS
TEL 01496 810441 WEBSITE www.bowmore.com VC

Evocative names like Dawn, Dusk, Voyage, and Legend accentuate the dream-like nature of the place. The village of Bowmore is the "capital" of Islay, but barely more than a hamlet, where the river Laggan flows into Lochindaal. On the edge of the boggy moor, the round church looks down the hill to the harbour.

The distillery, founded in 1779, is kept in beautiful condition – but not to be confused with the local school, which has decorative pagodas. In both geography and palate, the whiskies of Bowmore are between the intense malts of the south shore and the gentlest extremes of the north. Their character is not a compromise but an enigma, and tasters have found it difficult to unfold its complexity. The water used rises from iron-tinged rock, and picks up some peat from the earth as it flows by way of the Laggan, through moss, ferns, and rushes, to the distillery. While the peat higher on the island is rooty, that at Bowmore is sandier.

The company has its own maltings, where the peat is crumbled before it is fired to give more smoke than heat. The malt is peated for a shorter time than that used for the more intense Islay whiskies. Up to 30 per cent of the whisky is aged in sherry. The distillery is more exposed to the westerly winds than others, so there may be more ozone in the complex of aromas and flavours.

HOUSE STYLE Smoky, with leafy notes (ferns?) and sea air.
Younger ages before dinner, older after.

EXPRESSIONS WITH NO AGE STATEMENT
BOWMORE Legend, 40 vol

A light, young version, identified in some markets as an eight-year-old.

COLOUR Full gold.

NOSE Firm, peaty, smoky, very appetizing.

BODY Slightly sharp.

PALATE Very singular flavours, deftly balanced: a touch of iron,
leafy, ferny, peaty. Underlying earthy sweetness.
A fresh, young whisky, but no obvious spiritiness.

FINISH Sweet, then salty.

SCORE **80**

BOWMORE Surf, 43 vol

COLOUR Bright gold.

NOSE Fresh peat smoke.

BODY Light but smooth.

PALATE Light, dry, some nutty malt. A light, smooth, entry-level Bowmore.
Seems very tame at first, with a cookie-like maltiness, but the characteristic
ferny lavender, fragrant smoke and sea air gradually emerges.
One of the sweeter Bowmores.

FINISH Sweet smokiness. With water, later saltiness, honey-roast peanuts.

SCORE **78**

BOWMORE Dusk, Bordeaux (Claret) Wine Casked, 50 vol

This is a wine finish.

COLOUR Seems fractionally paler than claret finish. Orangey.

NOSE Seems slightly smokier than the version labelled Bowmore Claret.
Peaty. Leathery. Deliciously evocative and appetizing.

BODY Chewy.

PALATE Rich, fruity, smoky. Lots of flavour development: fruit,
nuts (almonds?), vanilla.

FINISH Toffeeish, oaky, smoky. Long.

SCORE **86**

BRUICHLADDICH

PRODUCER The Bruichladdich Distillery Co. Ltd
REGION Islay DISTRICT Loch Indaal
ADDRESS Bruichladdich, Islay, Argyll, PA49 7UN
TEL 01496 850221 WEBSITE www.bruichladdich.com
EMAIL laddie@bruichladdich.com VC

ISLANDERS CARRIED CHILDREN on their shoulders to witness the historic moment. They lined the Islay shore to watch the reopening in 2001 of Bruichladdich, Scotland's most westerly distillery. The single morning plane, bringing more guests, was running late. The people on the shore scanned the skies. They had waited ten years; what was another hour? Lovers of Bruichladdich had come from London, Seattle, and Tokyo. There were tears of joy, a ceilidh, and fireworks at midnight.

The new owners, headed by Mark Reynier, of the London wine merchants La Reserve, bought the distillery with plenty of maturing stock. Like many distilleries, Bruichladdich has a miscellany of former bourbon barrels and sherry butts, some containing their first fill of Scotch whisky, others their second or third. In any distillery, the selection of casks to make a bottling is critical. On the new team at Bruichladdich, this task is in the hands of one of the principals, veteran Islay whisky maker Jim McEwan. In his early vattings, McEwan has juggled casks to shake off the notion that Bruichladdich is almost too mild to be an Islay whisky.

The whisky has long combined light, firm maltiness with suggestions of passion fruit, seaweed, and salt. McEwan has coaxed out more fruitiness and some sweetness, and has given everything more life and definition. The latter qualities are heightened by the use of the distillery's own water in reduction and by the lack of chill filtration. These changes in procedure were made possible by the installation in 2003 of a bottling line. Bruichladdich thus becomes the third distillery to have its own bottling line on site. (The others are Springbank and Glenfiddich/Balvenie.)

The new range began with whiskies at 10, 15, 17, and 20 years old. As these are vatted from stock, their ages will increase over the next decade, until spirit distilled by the new team is ready. An annual vintage is also being released, and a bottling of yet older whiskies under the rubric Legacy. Yet further ranges are planned – under the rubrics Links and Full Strength. At the distillery, visitors who wish to buy a bottle are invited to sample from three current casks. The visitors bottle their own whiskies, under the rubric Valinch. This refers to the oversized pipette that is used in distilleries to remove samples from casks. This device is sometimes known as a "thief".

When Bruichladdich reopened, McEwan immediately reset the stills to produce a spirit to his requirements. This will remain light to medium in its peating. Two new spirits were added, with a heavier peating.

Bruichladdich (pronounced "brook laddie") is on the north shore of Lochindaal. The new owners have promoted the nickname "The Laddie", and introduced labels in a pale seaside blue to match the paintwork at the distillery. The distillery's water rises from iron-tinged stone, and flows lightly over peat. Unlike the other Islay distilleries, Bruichladdich is separated from the sea loch, albeit only by a quiet, coastal road.

The distillery was founded in 1881, rebuilt in 1886 and, despite an extension in 1975, remains little changed. All maturing spirit in its ownership is warehoused on the island, either at Bruichladdich or in the vestiges of the Lochindaal distillery, at Port Charlotte, the nearest village. Some independent bottlers of Bruichladdich have labelled the whisky Lochindaal.

The name Port Charlotte will be used on one of the new heavily peated spirits from Bruichladdich. An even peatier whisky will be called Octomore, after another former distillery at Port Charlotte. Parts of that distillery survive as Octomore Farm, home of Port Charlotte's lighthouse keeper, fire fighter and lifeboatman – who was also one of the pipers on the opening day at Bruichladdich.

HOUSE STYLE Light to medium, very firm, hint of passion fruit, salty, spicy (mace?). Very drinkable. Aperitif.

BRUICHLADDICH 10-year-old, 46 vol

COLOUR Bright greeny gold.

NOSE Fresh, clean. Very soft "sea air". Wild flowers among
the dunes. A picnic at the beach.

BODY Satin.

PALATE Summer fruits. Passion fruit. Zesty, almost
effervescent, Bruichladdich at its fruitiest.

FINISH The flavours meld, with a late frisson of sharpness.

SCORE *82*

BRUICHLADDICH 15-year-old, 46 vol

COLOUR Bright yellow.

NOSE Sea air. Perfumy. Slightly sharp.

BODY Firm, cracker-like, malt background.

PALATE Starts with a clean, grassy sweetness, then manifests an
astonishingly long, lively series of small explosions. Peppery.

FINISH Underlying iron. Savoury. Appetizing.

SCORE *80*

BRUICHLADDICH 17-year-old, 46 vol

COLOUR Deep gold, with green tinge.

NOSE Firm, confident, fruity. Passion fruit and sea air.

BODY Firm. Very dry.

PALATE Powerful. Long, sustained development of fruity,
estery flavours.

FINISH Iron. Salt. Muscular. Stimulating.

SCORE *83*

CAOL ILA

PRODUCER Diageo
REGION Islay DISTRICT North shore
ADDRESS Port Askaig, Islay, Argyll, PA46 7RL
TEL 01496 302760 Distillery has shop
WEBSITE www.discovering-distilleries.com/www.malts.com

A T THE ISLAY FESTIVAL OF 2002, three stylishly boxed expressions of Caol Ila were released by owners Diageo. Public attending the festival were invited to join whisky writers at the tasting. The tools of modern marketing were much in evidence, but so was the patrimony of Islay malt. Manager Billy Stichell, an Ileach, with four generations of family in the industry, provided an accomplished commentary. It was the first time he had spoken in public.

The launch of Caol Ila in an official bottling, in such a public way, and implicitly as the flagship in the new range, finally confirmed that it was far from hidden. Its malts had become more readily available, and appreciated, in recent years.

The name, pronounced "cull-eela", means "Sound of Islay". The Gaelic word "caol" is more familiar as "kyle". The distillery is in a cove near Port Askaig. The large windows of the still-house overlook the Sound of Islay, across which the ferry chugs to the nearby island of Jura. The best view of the distillery is from the ferry.

Inside, the distillery is both functional and attractive: a copper hood on the lauter tun; brass trim; wash stills like flat onions, spirit stills more pear-shaped; Oregon pine washbacks. Some of the structure dates from 1879, and the distillery was founded in 1846.

Behind the distillery, a hillside covered in fuchsias, foxgloves, and wild roses rises toward the peaty loch where the water gathers. It is quite salty and minerally, having risen from limestone. As a modern, well-engineered distillery, making whisky for several blends, it has over the years used different levels of peating. This is apparent in the independent bottlings.

HOUSE STYLE Oily, olive-like. Junipery, fruity, estery. A wonderful aperitif.

THE HIDDEN MALTS

CAOL ILA 12-year-old, 43 vol

COLOUR Vinho verde.

NOSE Soft. Juniper. Garden mint. Grass. Burnt grass.

BODY Lightly oily. Simultaneously soothing and appetizing.

PALATE Lots of flavour development. Becoming spicy. Vanilla, nutmeg, white mustard. Complex. Flavours combine with great delicacy.

FINISH Very long.

SCORE **83**

CAOL ILA 18-year-old, 43 vol

COLOUR Fullest of the three. Fino sherry on a sunny day.

NOSE Fragrant. Menthol. Markedly vegetal. Nutty vanilla pod.

BODY Firmer. Much bigger.

PALATE More assertively expressive. Sweeter. Leafy sweetness. Spring greens. Crushed almonds. Rooty, cedary.

FINISH Powerful reverberations of a remarkable whisky.

SCORE **86**

CAOL ILA Cask Strength, 55 vol

COLOUR Palest of the three, remarkably pale. White wine.

NOSE Intense. Sweetish, smokiness. Coconut. Grapefruit.

PALATE A very lively interplay of flavours, with malty sweetness fruity esteriness and peppery dryness. Perfumy, with suggestions of thyme.

FINISH The flavours come together in a rousing finale, with the alcohol providing a back beat.

SCORE **85**

SOME EARLIER OFFICIAL BOTTLINGS, NOW HARD TO FIND

CAOL ILA 15-year-old, Flora and Fauna, 43 vol

COLOUR Fino sherry, bright.

NOSE Aromatic, complex.

BODY Light, very firm, smooth.

PALATE Rounder, with the flavours more combined.

FINISH Oily and warming enough to keep out the sea.

SCORE **80**

CARDHU/CARDOW

PRODUCER Diageo
REGION Highlands DISTRICT Speyside
ADDRESS Aberlour, Banffshire, AB38 7RY
TEL 01340 872555 WEBSITE www.discovering-distilleries.com VC

A CONTROVERSIAL CHANGE, seen by some whisky lovers as a threat to the future of single malts, lay behind the adjustment to this distillery's name in 2003.

Such a threat could not issue from a less congruous location. Cardow has several claims to renown. It provided the industry with a dynastic family, the Cummings, and contributed twice to the tradition of strong women running distilleries. Helen Cummings distilled illegally on the family farm. Her daughter-in-law, Elizabeth, developed the legal distillery, which produced malt whisky as a substantial component of the Johnnie Walker blends.

The distillery was founded as Cardow (Gaelic for "black rock", after a nearby point on the river Spey). An alternative spelling, "Cardhu", better reflecting the pronunciation, was adopted when the distillery began to promote a bottled single malt. This mild, easily drinkable whisky was launched to compete with the popular malts in the early days of consumer interest.

It was a modest success in the United Kingdom, but enjoyed far greater sales in new markets for malts, such as France and Spain. In the latter country, the distinction between malts and blends seems to engage the consumer less than the age statement. Cardhu found itself head to head with the blend Chivas Regal, both being 12 years old. The Spaniards' taste for Scotch whisky is so great that the success of Cardhu in that market rendered it the world's fastest growing malt, outstripping the capacity of the distillery. Rather than "rationing" Cardhu, or increasing its price, owners Diageo decided to drop the designation "single" malt and substitute the imprecise "pure". Thus Cardhu was consumed by its own success.

The distillery, having reverted to the name Cardow, continues to produce whisky for bottling as Cardhu, but this is augmented by other Speyside distilleries under the same ownership.

Had Cardhu never been the name of a distillery and a single malt, there would be no cause for concern. Given that Cardhu was a single malt for between 30 and 40 years, and is now merely "pure" (meaning, in this instance, a vatted malt), there is a risk of confusion. The singularity of the name has been compromised, however good the "pure" malt.

How good, in this instance, is the pure malt? It seems a very good match, perhaps fractionally bigger: darker, oilier, nuttier, and drier. Initially, the only other component whisky to have been identified is Glendullan, but there are at least two others.

Diageo concedes the danger of confusion, and has worked hard to steer clear, but does not rule out more such transformations. If a single malt can, without changing its name, become less singular, how long before devotees become sceptics?

Other drinks try to set apart something special: microbrewed beers, real ales, first-growth clarets, Napoleon brandies, ... but none is as clearly defined as a single malt. It would be monumentally foolish to squander that advantage. The tasting notes below refer to Cardhu as a single malt.

HOUSE STYLE In the original form: light, smooth, delicate; an easy-drinking malt. Greater ages are richer, more toffeeish, and often work well with desserts.

CARDHU 12-year-old, 40 vol
Was widely distributed, and therefore still to be found,
though it has been replaced by Cardhu Pure Malt.

COLOUR Pale.

NOSE Light, appetizing, hints of greengage, and the gentlest touch of smoke.

BODY Light and smooth.

PALATE Light to medium in flavour, with the emphasis on malty sweetness and vanilla.

FINISH A lingering, syrupy sweetness, but also a rounder dryness with late hints of peat, although again faint.

SCORE 72

CLYNELISH

PRODUCER Diageo
REGION Highlands   DISTRICT Northern Highlands
ADDRESS Brora, Sutherland, KW9 6LR
TEL 01408 623003
WEBSITE www.discovering-distilleries.com/www.malts.com   VC

CULT STATUS SEEMS TO have been conferred in recent years on the Clynelish distillery and its adjoining predecessor, Brora, which command the middle stretch of the northern Highlands.

The appeal of their malts lies partly in their coastal aromas and flavours. Sceptics may question the brineyness of coastal malts, but some bottlings of Brora and Clynelish make that characteristic hard to deny. They are the most maritime of the East Coast malts, and on the Western mainland are challenged only by Springbank.

For a time, the big flavours of Clynelish and Brora were heightened by the use of well-peated malts. Clynelish cultists are always keen to identify distillates from this period. A similar preoccupation is to distinguish malts made at the Brora distillery from those that were distilled at Clynelish.

The two distilleries stand next door to each other on a landscaped hillside near the fishing and golfing resort of Brora. They overlook the coastal road as it heads toward the northernmost tip of the Scottish mainland.

The older of the two distilleries was built in 1819 by the Duke of Sutherland to use grain grown by his tenants. This distillery was originally known as Clynelish: the first syllable rhymes with "wine", the second with "leash". The name means "slope of the garden". After a century and half, a new Clynelish was built in 1967–68, but demand was sufficient for the two distilleries to operate in tandem for a time. They were initially known as Clynelish 1 and 2. Eventually, the older distillery was renamed Brora. It worked sporadically until 1983.

Brora is a traditional 19th-century distillery, in local stone (now overgrown), with a pagoda. Clynelish's stills greet the world through the floor-to-ceiling windows, in the classic design of the period, with a fountain to soften the façade.

Inside, the still-house has its own peculiarities, in which the deposits in the low wines and feints receivers play a part. The result is an oily, beeswax background flavour – another distinctive feature.

For years, this robustly distinctive malt was available only as a 12-year-old, bearing a charmingly amateurish label, from Ainslie and Heilbron, a DCL subsidiary, whose blends were given brand names of equal charm. The Real McTavish was a good example. Since the United Distillers and Diageo eras, Brora and Clynelish have been positively anthologous. Editions have been issues by Flora and Fauna, The Rare Malts, Cask Strength Limited Editions, Hidden Malts, as well as Special Releases.

HOUSE STYLE Seaweedy, spicy. Mustard-and-oil.
With a roast-beef sandwich.

CLYNELISH, 14-year-old, 46 vol, Hidden Malts
*Replaces more seaweedy Flora and Fauna edition reviewed in
the fourth edition of Malt Whisky Companion.*

COLOUR Bright pale orange.

NOSE Fragrant. A stroll in the sand dunes.

BODY Firm, oily and seductively smoky.

PALATE Firm hit of cleansing flavours. Coriander. Orange. Dry. Spicy.
Distinctively mustardy.

FINISH The spiciness becomes yet more perfumy and exotic.
Both satisfying (without being satiating).

SCORE 81

BRORA 1977, 24-year-old, Cask Strength, The Rare Malts, 56.1 vol

COLOUR Very bright primrose. Lime tinge?

NOSE Very flowery. Camomile. Suggestion of sweet lime.

BODY Lightly oily.

PALATE Lively, fruity, refreshing. Distinctive gorse or whin; that coconut flavour. Then fresh lime, then peppery seaweed.

FINISH Sandy, grainy, mustardy. Wasabi?
Does the 18th hole at Brora serve sushi?

SCORE **84**

BRORA 30-year-old, Special Release, Limited Bottling of 3000, 52.4 vol

COLOUR Greeny gold.

NOSE Fruity. Fresh limes. Indian lime pickle.

BODY Light but firm.

PALATE Powerfully peaty, with "island" flavours of spinach-like seaweed, salt and pepper.

FINISH Stingingly mustardy. Joyously extrovert.

SCORE **86**

EARLIER "OFFICIAL" BOTTLINGS

A 1982 Clynelish at 57.7 vol, in the Cask Strength series of Limited Editions, was assertive, seaweedy and slightly metallic. SCORE 81

A 1975 Brora, at 20 years and 59.1 vol, also in the Rare Malts series, had an intensely flowery aroma; a flowery, seaweedy, medicinal palate; and iodine, seaweed and salt in its long, lingering finish. A classic. SCORE 84

A 1977 Brora, at 21 years and 56.9 vol, in the Rare Malts series, had a good maritime character and a distinctively tar-like note. SCORE 85

A 1972 Clynelish, at 22 years and 58.95 vol, in the Rare Malts series, had more spice. Earlier Rare Malts from Brora have included a more flowery 1975. SCORE 84

There was also a wonderfully seaweedy, medicinal 1972. SCORE 86

CONVALMORE

PRODUCER William Grant & Sons Ltd
REGION Highlands DISTRICT Speyside (Dufftown)
ADDRESS Dufftown, Banffshire, AB55 4BD

A RARE MALT OF Convalmore from Diageo in 2003 was something of a surprise – and a very pleasant one, given the quality of the whisky. The pagodas of Dufftown make an impressive congregation of landmarks, and Convalmore's is one of the most strikingly visible. Sadly, the distillery no longer operates.

For much of its life, Convalmore contributed malt whisky to the Buchanan/Black & White blends. The distillery was built in the 1870s; seriously damaged by fire, and rebuilt in 1910; modernized in 1964–65, but mothballed a couple of decades later by its owners at the time, DCL. Their successors, Diageo, still have the right to issue bottlings of Convalmore whisky from stock. In 1992, the premises were acquired by William Grant & Sons, owners of nearby Glenfiddich and Balvenie, but purely as warehousing.

HOUSE STYLE Malty, syrupy, fruity, biggish.
After dinner.

CONVALMORE 1981, Signatory, 43 vol

COLOUR *Eau-de-nil.*

NOSE Aromatic. Perfumy. Lavender. Wild mint.

BODY Very silky.

PALATE Fleshy. Musky. White rum. Cocoa butter. Pralines.
Mint chocolates.

FINISH Fresh, clean, stinging.

SCORE 71

CONVALMORE 1978, 24-year-old,
Rare Malt, 59.4 vol

COLOUR Shimmery pale gold.

NOSE Gently sweet. Oily cereal character. A fresh day on Speyside,
with a little smoke wafting quickly past.

BODY Medium. Creamy. Syrupy.

PALATE Chocolate cream in a cookie sandwich. Becoming less
chocolatey, more biscuity and drier.

FINISH Fruity. Lemon pith. Slightly woody. Alcoholic. Warming.
Long. Powerful.

SCORE 79

CONVALMORE 1977, 21-year-old,
Cadenhead, 64.4 vol

COLOUR Old gold. Dusty, full gold.

NOSE Oily. Passion fruit. Iron-ish, but sweet.

BODY Drying on the tongue. Clinging syrupiness.

PALATE Gritty. Dry. Sherbety. Peppery.

FINISH Big, long, rummy, warming syrupiness. After dinner.

SCORE 75

CONVALMORE 1960, Gordon & MacPhail, 40 vol

Released in 1999 as part of a new Rare Old series.

COLOUR Rich, lemony gold.

NOSE Aromatic. Oily. Very "clean" smoke.

BODY Medium. Oily. Clean.

PALATE Begins with a good malt background. Distinctly oily.
Again, lightly smoky.

FINISH Light malt. Hint of honey. Yet more oiliness. Hint of sulphur.
Clean peatiness. Warming. Long.

SCORE 70

CRAGGANMORE

PRODUCER Diageo
REGION Highlands DISTRICT Speyside
ADDRESS Ballindalloch, Banffshire, AB37 9AB TEL 01479 8747000
WEBSITE www.discovering-distilleries.com/www.malts.com

A WONDERFULLY COMPLEX SPECIAL RELEASE in 2003 demonstrated what a great malt this is. Cragganmore is still less widely known than might be expected. The distillery, founded in 1869–70, is very pretty, hidden in a hollow high on the Spey. Its water, from nearby springs, is relatively hard, and its spirit stills have an unusual, flat-topped shape. These two elements may be factors in the complexity of the malt. The usual version, from refill sherry casks, some more sherried independent bottlings, and the port finish, are each in their own ways almost equal delights. Cragganmore is a component of Old Parr.

HOUSE STYLE Austere, stonily dry, aromatic. After dinner.

CRAGGANMORE 12-year-old, 40 vol

COLOUR Golden.

NOSE The most complex aroma of any malt. Its bouquet is astonishingly fragrant and delicate, with sweetish notes of cut grass and herbs (thyme perhaps?).

BODY Light to medium, but very firm and smooth.

PALATE Delicate, clean, restrained, with a huge range of herbal, flowery notes.

FINISH Long.

SCORE 90

CRAGGANMORE 1984, Double Matured, 40 vol

Finished in ruby port.

COLOUR Pale amber.

NOSE Heather honey. Scented. Beeswax. Hessian.

BODY Firm, smooth. Fuller.

PALATE Flowery. Orange blossom. Sweet oranges. Cherries. Port.

FINISH Flowery, balancing dryness. Warming. Soothing.

Connoisseurs might miss the austerity of the original – or enjoy the added layer of fruity, winey sweetness.

SCORE 90

CRAGGANMORE 1973, 29-year-old, Special Release Issued 2003, 52.5 vol

COLOUR Gold, with a faint green tinge.

NOSE Fragrant, grassy, herbal, with both dryness and sweetness.

BODY Soft, slightly oily, dry.

PALATE Dry notes like bison grass, thyme and pepper, but also sweeter flavours like liquorice and orange blossom.

FINISH Long, dry, flowery, cleansing.

SCORE 92

SOME INDEPENDENT BOTTLINGS OF CRAGGANMORE:

Murray McDavid's bottling of a cask from 1990 at 46 vol is pale straw in colour. A subtle refined nose hinting at berry fruits, mandarin, dried apple, white pepper and a grassy note. Medium weight. The palate is slightly flat. SCORE 80.

A 1989 bottling from Blackadder at 59.6 vol is light gold in colour; water brings out slightly grubby wood. The palate and body shows a light whisky which has had little interaction with the cask. SCORE 70

Signatory's 1989, 55.7 vol, is light gold with a nose of powdered almond, sultana, and suggestions of weight; the palate is soft and sweet with good character, but lacks the depth of the official bottlings. SCORE 83

DAILUAINE

PRODUCER Diageo
REGION Highlands DISTRICT Speyside
ADDRESS Carron, Aberlour, Banffshire, AB38 7RE
TEL 01340 872500

Between the mountain Ben Rinnes and the river Spey, at the hamlet of Carron, not far from Aberlour, the Dailuaine ("Dal-oo-ayn") distillery is hidden in a hollow. The name means "green vale", and that accurately describes the setting. It was founded in 1852, and has been rebuilt several times since.

It is one of several distilleries along the Spey valley that once had its own railway halt for workers and visitors – and as a means of shipping in barley or malt and despatching the whisky. A small part of the Speyside line still runs trains for hobbyists and visitors, at the Aviemore ski resort, and Dailuaine's own shunting locomotive has appeared there under steam, but is now preserved at Aberfeldy, a distillery formerly in the same group. Most of the route from the mountains to the sea is now preserved for walkers, as the Speyside Way. Dailuaine's whisky has long been a component of the Johnnie Walker blends. It was made available as a single malt in the Flora and Fauna series in 1991, and later in a Cask Strength Limited Edition.

HOUSE STYLE Firmly malty, fruity, fragrant.
After dinner.

DAILUAINE 16-year-old, Flora and Fauna, 43 vol

COLOUR Emphatically reddish amber.

NOSE Sherryish but dry, perfumy.

BODY Medium to full, smooth.

PALATE Sherryish, with barley-sugar maltiness, but balanced by a dry cedar or oak background.

FINISH Sherryish, smooth, very warming, long.

SCORE **76**

THE DALMORE

PRODUCER Whyte and MacKay Ltd
REGION Highlands   DISTRICT Northern Highlands
ADDRESS Alness, Morayshire, IV17 0UT
TEL 01349 882362   WEBSITE www.dalmoredistillery.co.uk

A RECORD PRICE FOR A BOTTLE OF WHISKY was established in 2002, when a Dalmore 62-year-old single malt was sold at auction to an anonymous bidder for just over £25,000/$38,000. Records are made to be broken, but this was a timely boost to the distillery, not long returned to Scottish ownership. The record-breaking sale took place at McTear's, the Glasgow auction house. The whisky was vatted from vintages of 1868, 1878, 1926, and 1939. Over the years, it had been racked several times, latterly in an oloroso sherry butt from Gonzalez Byass.

The man who makes the vattings and blendings for Whyte and Mackay, Richard Patterson, is one of the industry's extroverts. He may well have celebrated with a cigar. One of his creations is Dalmore The Cigar Malt, a rich whisky intended to accompany a fine Havana. It is easy to imagine the finest cigars being smoked in the oak-panelled offices at Dalmore. The panels previously graced a shooting lodge.

Dalmore, said to have been founded in 1839, was once owned by a distinguished local family, the Mackenzies, friends of James Whyte and Charles Mackay, who created a famous name in blended Scotch. Latterly, the proprietor was Jim Beam, of Kentucky. The management buy-out of Jim Beam's Scottish distilleries led to the restoration of the Whyte and Mackay name.

Dalmore has an unusual still-house. The wash stills have a conical upper chamber and the spirit stills are cooled with a water jacket – another distinctive feature. There are two pairs of stills, identical in shape but different sizes. The warehouses are by the waters of the Cromarty Firth. About 85 per cent of the whisky is matured in bourbon casks, mainly first-fill, the rest in sweet oloroso and amontillado, but it is all married in sherry butts.

HOUSE STYLE Rich, flavourful, orange marmalade. After dinner.

THE DALMORE 12-year-old, 40 vol

COLOUR An attractive amber hue.

NOSE Arousing, with rum butter, malt loaf, and soda bread.

BODY Medium. Silky smooth.

PALATE Gradual flavour development. Malty sweetness,
orange jelly beans, spiciness (anise?), perfuminess, heather,
light peat Even a faint, salty tang of the sea.

FINISH Toasty. Grainy, Long

SCORE **79**

THE DALMORE "Black Isle", 12-year old, 43 vol

COLOUR Slightly darker and redder. Copper.

NOSE More obvious sherry. Apricot jam. Morello cherries. Pipe tobacco.

BODY Velvety.

PALATE Seville oranges. Candied orange peels in mincemeat. Mince pies.

FINISH Rooty. Liquorice. Lingering.

SCORE **80**

THE DALMORE Cigar Malt, 40 vol

*A marriage of Dalmore whiskies between ten and 20 years old,
mainly in the-mid teens.*

COLOUR Dark orange.

NOSE A soft smokiness. Suggestions of black chocolate and orange creams.

BODY Firm.

PALATE Rich, rounded. A hint of rum butter, then dryish and firm.
Hard caramel toffee. Hint of burnt sugar. Faint smoke. Never cloying.
With the cigar, a complement rather than a contrast.

FINISH Light, smoky, wood bark, ground almonds, dryness. Scores points
for originality and for balance.

SCORE **81**

DALWHINNIE

PRODUCER Diageo
REGION Highlands   DISTRICT Speyside
ADDRESS Dalwhinnie, Inverness-shire, PH19 1AB
TEL 01540 672219   VC
WEBSITE www.discovering-distilleries.com/www.malts.com

O NE OF THE HIGHEST DISTILLERIES in Scotland, at 326 metres (1073 feet), Dalwhinnie has the Monadhlaith Mountains to one side, and the Forest of Atholl, the Cairngorms, and the Grampians to the other. Its name is Gaelic for "meeting place". The village of the same name stands at the junction of old cattle-droving routes from the west and north down to the central Lowlands. Much whisky smuggling went on along this route. The distillery was called Strathspey when it opened in 1897. It is near the upper reaches of the Spey, although Dalwhinnie represents the Highlands in Diageo's Classic Malts range.

HOUSE STYLE Lightly peaty. Cut grass and heather honey. Clear flavours against a very clean background. Aperitif.

DALWHINNIE 15-year-old, 43 vol

COLOUR Bright gold.

NOSE Very aromatic, dry, faintly phenolic, lightly peaty.

BODY Firm, slightly oily.

PALATE Remarkably smooth, long-lasting flavour development. Aromatic, heather-honey notes give way to cut-grass, malty sweetness, which intensifies to a sudden burst of peat.

FINISH A long crescendo.

SCORE 76

DALWHINNIE 15-year-old,
Friends of the Classic Malts Bottling, 56.9 vol

COLOUR Light gold.

NOSE Hard to get much on nose: sulphur, guava, coconut cream. Alcohol.

BODY Light and delicate.

PALATE Delicate, but better weight than the nose suggests. Tropical fruit.
More about feel than aroma.

FINISH Crisp. Oaky.

SCORE **70**

DALWHINNIE 1980, Double Matured, 43 vol
Oloroso finish.

COLOUR Sunny gold to bronze.

NOSE Oloroso, liquorice, rooty, grassy.

BODY Firm, rounded.

PALATE Very sweet, toffeeish start. Honey. Lemons. Long flavour
development to peatiness, cut grass, vanilla, and fresh oak. Beautiful
interplay and balance. The sherry sweetness seems, by contrast, to
accentuate the usually light peatiness of Dalwhinnie.

FINISH Very long. Cut grass, peat, smoke, oak.

SCORE **79**

DALWHINNIE 1973, 29-year-old, Special Release of 2003, 57.8 vol

COLOUR Restrained, warm gold.

NOSE Appetizingly fruity. Lemon grass. Orange juice on breakfast pancakes.

BODY Smooth. Textured.

PALATE Bursts with fruitiness. Apples, bananas?
Against cereal-grain background.

FINISH Refreshing. Lively. Scenty.

SCORE **78**

DALWHINNIE 1966, 36-year-old, Limited Bottling of 1500,
Bottled 2002, 47.2 vol

COLOUR Full gold. Hint of bronze.

NOSE Aromatic. Oily. Restrained peat. Some grassy, moorland aromas.

BODY Very light. As fresh as spring water.

PALATE Clean, very firm maltiness. Honey-glazed biscuits.
Pronounced vanilla. Slowly developing lively, appetizing moorland grass
and faint smokiness.

FINISH Very long and warming.

SCORE **79**

DUFFTOWN

PRODUCER Diageo
REGION Highlands   DISTRICT Speyside (Dufftown)
ADDRESS Dufftown, Keith, Banffshire, AB55 4BR
TEL 01340 822100   WEBSITE www.malts.com

THE EARL OF FIFE, James Duff, laid out this handsome, hilly little town of stone buildings in 1817. The town's name is pronounced "duff-ton". Dufftown lies at the confluence of the rivers Fiddich and Dullan on their way to the Spey. There are six active malt distilleries in the town; a further two survive as buildings but are highly unlikely ever to operate again. A ninth, Pittyvaich, has recently been bulldozed.

Only one of the distilleries appropriates Dufftown as its name. This distillery and Pittyvaich, its erstwhile next-door neighbour, were both owned by Bell's until that company was acquired by United Distillers, now Diageo. Dufftown's stone-built premises were a meal mill until 1896, but they have since sprouted a pagoda, and were twice expanded in the 1970s. They now comprise one of Diageo's larger distilleries, but most of its output goes into Bell's, the biggest selling blend in the UK.

HOUSE STYLE Aromatic, dry, malty. Aperitif.

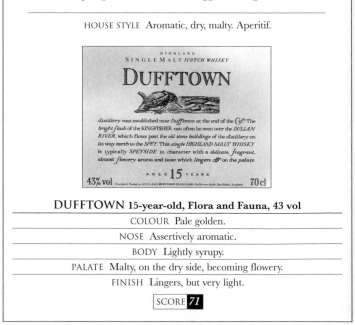

DUFFTOWN 15-year-old, Flora and Fauna, 43 vol

COLOUR Pale golden.

NOSE Assertively aromatic.

BODY Lightly syrupy.

PALATE Malty, on the dry side, becoming flowery.

FINISH Lingers, but very light.

SCORE **71**

GLEN ELGIN

PRODUCER Diageo
REGION Highlands DISTRICT Speyside (Lossie)
ADDRESS Longmorn, Elgin, Morayshire, IV30 3SL
TEL 01343 862000

A "HIDDEN MALTS" BOTTLING, at 12 years old, is a welcome response to those who have urged that this classic Speyside whisky be more readily available as a single. There had previously been a version at around the same level of maturity, but without an age statement. This had been marketed mainly in Japan. The newer expression seems more flowery and complex, while the previous version was more winey.

The distillery itself has never been hidden, but it was for some years heavily branded with the name White Horse, in recognition of its contribution to that blend. The Glen Elgin distillery is very visible on one of the main roads into the town whose name it bears. Although it is just over a hundred years old, its façade dates from 1964, and reflects the classic DCL still-house design of the period.

Where the River Lossie approaches the town of Elgin, there are no fewer than eight distilleries within a few miles. Elgin is also worth a visit for Gordon & MacPhail's whisky shop as well as 13th-century cathedral ruins.

HOUSE STYLE Honey and tangerines. Restorative or after dinner.

GLEN ELGIN 12 year-old, Hidden Malts, 43 vol

COLOUR Deep gold.

NOSE Fruity and flowery. Heather honey. Pears poached in spices.
Hint of coffee beans.

BODY Light but firm.

PALATE Fresh and crisp, flowery, and gingery. A touch of mandarin.

FINISH Dry and spicy.

SCORE 77

GLEN ELGIN Centenary, 19-year-old, 60 vol

Bottle 297 of 750 to commemorate the first distillation on 1 May 1900.

COLOUR Pale amber, pinkish tinge.

NOSE Flowery heather honey, with spicy, cedary, oaky notes.

BODY Textured.

PALATE Warm honey. Seville orange. Toasted nuts.
Beautifully rounded. Elegant.

FINISH Fragrant. Long and creamy. Delicate smokiness.

SCORE 82

GLEN ELGIN 32-year-old, Distilled 1971, Special Release 2003, 42.3 vol

COLOUR Full gold.

NOSE Fragrant. Cedary. Honeyed. Seductive.

BODY Soft, rich, tongue-coating.

PALATE Clean, sweet. A hint of Seville orange. Intense heather honey.
Cereal grain. Crunchy. A lovely whisky.

FINISH Gently drying. Shortbread.

SCORE 81

GLEN ELGIN 1968, Gordon & MacPhail, 40 vol

COLOUR Deep old gold.

NOSE Distinctively sherry. Exotic wood. Rich sweetness.
Candied orange. Crème brûlée.

BODY Medium, velvety.

PALATE Lusciously smooth. Oak and fruit elegantly mingled.
A touch of cinnamon.

FINISH Dry but rich and long. Hint of bitter chocolate.

SCORE 77

GLEN MHOR

PRODUCER DCL
REGION Highlands   DISTRICT Speyside (Inverness)
SITE OF FORMER DISTILLERY Telford Street, Inverness, Inverness-shire, IV3 5LU

Purists pronounce it the Gaelic way, "Glen Vawr", to rhyme with "law". The distillery, built in 1892 in Inverness and demolished in 1986, was one of several at which the poet, novelist, and pioneering whisky writer, Neil Gunn, worked as an exciseman. In his book, *Scotch Missed*, Brian Townsend writes that Gunn was inspired by Glen Mhor to let slip his observation that "until a man has had the luck to chance upon a perfectly matured malt, he does not really know what whisky is". Even in Gunn's day, Glen Mhor could be found as a single malt, and casks still find their way into independent bottlings.

HOUSE STYLE Aromatic, treacly. Quite sweet. With dessert or after dinner.

GLEN MHOR, 22-year-old, Distilled 1979, Bottled 2001, Rare Malts, 61 vol

COLOUR Shimmery old gold.

NOSE Surprisingly fresh, minty, and herbal.

BODY Lightly syrupy. Texture reminiscent of whipped cream.
Rose-water, sherbet. Meringue on a shortbread base.

FINISH Distinctly leafy and grassy.

SCORE 78

THE SINGLETON OF GLEN ORD

PRODUCER UDV (Diageo)
REGION Highlands DISTRICT Northern Highlands
ADDRESS Muir of Ord, Ross-shire, IV6 7UJ TEL 01463 872008
WEBSITE www.discovering-distilleries.com/www.malts.com VC

THE NATIONAL POET, Robert Burns, albeit a Lowlander, had a taste for this corner of the Northern Highlands. The peninsula known as the Black Isle grows fine malting barley, the "blood" of which (to use Burns' thirsty word) ascended to the spirit world at Ferintosh (Scotland's first commercial distillery, long gone and lamented by Burns).

The maltings (of the drum type) at Muir of Ord serves the adjoining distillery and several others. The distillery, established in 1837/8, was rebuilt in 1966. Having barley that is grown and malted in the area renders this something of an "estate" distillery. I have long enjoyed its whisky. Why isn't it better known? "An under-rated distillery," I pronounced in 1989, in the first edition of the Malt Whisky Companion. I felt the whisky's image had been confused by the constant tampering with its name. It has been variously labelled as Ord, Ordie, Glen Ordie and Muir of Ord. The latter, meaning "The Moor by the Hill", is the name of the nearby village. The Singleton bottlings released in 2006 and reviewed below have considerably more sherry character than some of the earlier expressions. Opinions are divided, but to my taste, this greatly extends and highlights the full flavours of these whiskies, and makes for seductive, devilish, drams.

HOUSE STYLE Flavoursome, rose-like, spicy (cinnamon?),
and malty, with a dry finish. After dinner.

THE SINGLETON OF GLEN ORD 12-year-old, 40 vol

Colour: Peach conserve on toast. Bright, iridescent, like the reflective sheen on a satin bedspread. Breakfast from room service. A hint of pink (The Financial Times, being read in bed?)

Nose: Sherry. Raisin. Prunes. Dried fruit with stalks. Fruity. Flaked almonds. Cereal grains.

Palate: Malay. Firm. Smooth. Hard toffee. Rose water. Peppermint. Almond pudding. Sophisticated, smooth, sensuous.

Finish: Bitter chocolate. Cinnamon. Perfume, fragrant. A wisp of smoke.

SCORE 80

THE SINGLETON OF GLEN ORD 18-year-old, 40 vol

Colour: Blood orange.

Nose: Perfumy. A fresh scent, like almond oil shampoo or shower gel. Then toasted almond croissants, filled with marzipan. Muesli. Dried figs.

Body: Oily, especially after water. Confectioners' marshmallow.

Palate Expensive biscuits (Chocolate Olivers? Duchy Originals?) coated with thick, hard, black chocolate, and with a filling like that in pralines. The "praline filling" develops from walnut to caramel to restrained ginger and finally coffee cream.

Finish: Long and beautifully rounded. Very gently warming. A hint of cinnamon and roses – and the slightest suggestion of phenol. Mature. Some sherry oakiness.

SCORE 81

GLEN SPEY

PRODUCER Diageo
REGION Highlands DISTRICT Speyside (Rothes)
ADDRESS Rothes, Aberlour, Banffshire, AB38 7AU
TEL 01340 882000

A FLORA AND FAUNA BOTTLING launched in 2002 renders this distillery slightly more visible. It is in the heart of Speyside, but not on the river. Glen Spey, dating from the 1880s, is in Rothes. Much of its whisky is destined for the house blend of an aristocratic wine and spirits merchant in St James's, London. (It is coincidence that neighbour Glenrothes follows a parallel path). In the case of Glen Spey, the merchant is Justerini & Brooks, whose house blend is J&B.

Giacomo Justerini was an Italian, from Bologna. He emigrated to Britain in pursuit of an opera singer, Margherita Bellion, in 1749. The romance does not seem to have come to fruition, but Justerini meanwhile worked in Britain as a maker of liqueurs. By 1779, he was already selling Scotch whisky. Brooks was a later partner in the firm. The business was for a time part of Gilbeys, at which point there was for a time a nutty, grassy eight-year-old Glen Spey.

HOUSE STYLE Light, grassy, nutty. Aperitif.

GLEN SPEY 12 year-old, Flora and Fauna, 43 vol

COLOUR Full gold.

NOSE Cookie-like maltiness (rich tea biscuit), dusty floor.
Kumquat. Leafy. Garden mint.

BODY Medium. Oily.

PALATE Vivacious. Starts intensely sweet, with light citrus notes,
then becomes dramatically drier.

FINISH Crisp. Lemon zest. Pith.

SCORE **75**

GLENDULLAN

PRODUCER Diageo
REGION Highland DISTRICT Speyside (Dufftown)
ADDRESS Dufftown, Banffshire, AB55 4DJ
TEL 01340 822100

NOW A CONTRIBUTOR to the vatted adaptation of Cardhu, and traditionally to the blend Old Parr, which is popular in Japan. As a single malt, Glendullan has in recent years been offered in a flora and fauna edition, and no fewer than four Rare Malts versions.

This distillery, established in 1897‑98, has had its moments of glory, notably the supply of its whisky in the early 1900s to King Edward VII, an honour that was for some years proclaimed on its casks. Today, Glendullan has the highest volume production among Diageo's distilleries, despite a name so unjustly close to "dull one". The reference is to the river Dullan, on which Dufftown stands.

HOUSE STYLE Perfumy, fruity, dry, chilli-like, oily, big. Put it in a hip flask.

GLENDULLAN 12-year-old, Flora and Fauna, 43 vol

COLOUR	Almost white, with just a tinge of gold.
NOSE	Light, dry maltiness. Hint of fruit.
BODY	A hard edge, then silky.
PALATE	Dry start, becoming buttery, malty, nutty, perfumy, and lightly fruity.
FINISH	Extraordinarily perfumy and long.

SCORE 75

GLENFIDDICH

PRODUCER William Grant & Sons Ltd
REGION Highlands DISTRICT Speyside (Dufftown)
ADDRESS Dufftown, Banffshire, AB55 4DH
TEL 01340 820373 VC WEBSITE www.glenfiddich.com

AS BOLD AND ADVENTUROUS as ever, the stag has been raising its antlers in the glen of the river Fiddich. Not only has the world's biggest selling single malt whisky increased the age of its principal expression, it has also introduced controversial innovations like Havana Reserve and Caoran.

The Glenfiddich distillery lies on the small river whose name it bears, in Dufftown. The name Fiddich indicates that the river runs through the valley of the deer. Hence the company's stag emblem.

This justifiably famous distillery was founded in 1886–87, and is still controlled by the original family. As a relatively small enterprise, it faced intense competition from bigger companies during the economic boom after the Second World War. Rather than relying on supplying whisky to blenders owned by the giants, it decided in 1963 to widen the availability of its whisky as a bottled single malt. An industry dominated at the time by blended Scotches regarded this as foolishness. The widely held view was that single malts were too intense, flavoursome, or complex for the English and other foreigners.

This independent spirit was an example without which few of its rivals would have been emboldened to offer themselves as bottled single malts. Devotees of the genre owe a debt of gratitude to Glenfiddich. The early start laid the foundations for the success of Glenfiddich. Its fortunes were no doubt further assisted by its being, among malts, very easily drinkable.

Devotees of malts who are ready for a greater challenge will find much more complexity in the longer matured versions, including the one that is aged for 15 years then vatted in a solera system.

The Glenfiddich distillery is full of character. Much of the original structure, in honey-and-grey stone, remains beautifully maintained, and the style has been followed in considerable new construction. Glenfiddich also led the way in the industry by being the first to have a visitor centre. Some may be argue that this is for tourists rather than purists, but no visitor to this part of the Highlands should miss it.

A truly traditional element is the use of coal firing in one of the two still-houses. The stills are small, and the whisky is principally aged in "plain oak" (refill bourbon), although about 10 per cent goes into sherry casks. Whisky aged in different woods is married in plain oak.

Adjoining the Glenfiddich site, William Grant also owns The Balvenie (established 1892), with a small floor maltings, and the newish (1990) Kininvie malt distilleries. Kininvie is little more than a basic still-house. Its rich, creamy malt goes into the Grant's blends, but has not been bottled as a single. Elsewhere in Scotland, it has the Girvan grain distillery.

HOUSE STYLE When young, a dry, fruity aperitif;
when more mature, a raisiny, chocolatey after-dinner malt.

GLENFIDDICH Special Reserve, 12-year-old, 40 vol

COLOUR Slightly fuller gold than it used to be. Faint green tinge.

NOSE Fresh but sweet, appetizing, fruity, pear-like, juicy grass.

BODY Lean. Smooth. Oily maltiness.

PALATE Malty sweetness. White chocolate. Good flavour
development. Toasted hazelnuts.

FINISH Fragrant suggestion of peat smoke.

SCORE **77**

GLENFIDDICH Caoran Reserve, 12-year-old, 40 vol

*Caoran refers in Gaelic to the embers of a peat fire. A very gently smoky,
dryish background is achieved by the use of casks that previously
contained whisky from the peaty island of Islay.*

COLOUR Deep gold.

NOSE Treacle toffee slightly burned. Sweet, cedary logs on a slow fire.

BODY Light to medium. Oily. Scented.

PALATE White chocolate. Cassata ice cream. Strega.

FINISH Thick chocolate wafers. Dark caramel. Gently warming alcohol.

SCORE **82**

GLENFIDDICH Solera Reserve, 15-year-old, 40 vol

COLOUR Bright gold.

NOSE Chocolate. Toast. Hint of peat.

BODY Light but very smooth indeed.

PALATE Suave. Silky. White chocolate. Pears in cream. Cardamom.

FINISH Cream. Hint of ginger.

SCORE **81**

GLENFIDDICH 15-year-old, Cask Strength, 51 vol

Especially available in duty-free.

COLOUR Full gold.

NOSE Soft, light peat smoke.

BODY Smooth, lightly creamy.

PALATE Smooth. Hazelnut. Light cream. Dry maltiness.

FINISH Tasty, appetizing. Grassy notes and peat smoke.

SCORE **80**

GLENFIDDICH Ancient Reserve, 18-year-old, 40 vol

A proportion of the whisky in this version is older than the age on the label, with a slight accent toward first-fill sherry (butts, rather than hogsheads, and made from Spanish oak rather than American), and earth-floored, traditional warehouses.

COLOUR Old gold.

NOSE Richer.

BODY Softer.

PALATE More mellow and rounded, soft, and restrained.
Scores points for sophistication and sherry character.

FINISH Nutty. A flowery hint of peat.

SCORE **78**

GLENFIDDICH Havana Reserve, 40 vol

To be renamed Gran Reserva.

COLOUR Apricot.

NOSE Toasty. Biscuity. Petit fours. The aroma when
a box of chocolates is opened.

BODY Soft. Lightly creamy.

PALATE Vanilla flan. Sweet Cuban coffee.

FINISH Juicy. A hint of dried tropical fruits.

SCORE **86**

GLENFIDDICH 30-year-old, 43 vol

COLOUR Full gold, fractionally darker still.

NOSE Notes of sherry, fruit, chocolate, and ginger.

BODY Soft, full, some viscosity.

PALATE More sherry, raisins, chocolate, ginger. Luxurious.

FINISH Unhurried, with chocolatey notes and gingery dryness.

SCORE **86**

GLENKINCHIE

PRODUCER Diageo
REGION Lowlands DISTRICT Eastern Lowlands
ADDRESS Pencaitland, Tranent, East Lothian, EH34 5ET
TEL 01875 342005
WEBSITE www.discovering-distilleries.com/www.malts.com VC

ACCORDING TO ITS LABEL, "The Edinburgh Malt". This is an eminently visitable distillery, about 25 kilometres (15 miles) from the capital, and near the village of Pencaitland. It traces its origins to at least the 1820s and 1830s, to a farm in barley-growing country in the glen of the Kinchie burn. This rises in the green Lammermuir hills, which provide medium-hard water, and flows toward the small coastal resorts where the Firth of Forth meets the sea.

In the 1940s and 1950s, the distillery manager bred prize-winning cattle, feeding them on the spent grain. Delphiniums and roses grow outside the manager's office, and the distillery has its own bowling green. The buildings resemble those of a Borders woollen mill. For much of the distillery's history, the whisky was largely used in the Haig blends. In 1988–89, it was launched as a single in the Classic Malts range, and in 1997 an amontillado finish was added. In the same year a new visitor centre was opened. Among the exhibits is a 75-year-old model of the distillery which was built by the firm of Basset-Lowke, better known for their miniature steam engines.

HOUSE STYLE Flowery start, complex flavours, and a dry finish.
A restorative, especially after a walk in the hills.

GLENKINCHIE 10-year-old, 43 vol

COLOUR Gold.

NOSE Softly aromatic. Lemon grass. Sweet lemons. Melons.

BODY Light but rounded.

PALATE Soft, spicy. Cinnamon and demerara, then gingery dryness.
An extraordinary interplay.

FINISH Fragrant, spicy, oaky dryness.

SCORE **76**

GLENKINCHIE 12-year-old, Friends of Classic Malts, 58.7 vol

COLOUR Bright gold.

NOSE Grass. Straw. Marshmallow. Lime jelly.

BODY Lightly creamy.

PALATE Smooth. Crème brûlée.

FINISH Finely grated lemon peel. Lemon grass. Root ginger.
Nutmeg. Spicy. Big. Long. Dryish.

SCORE **80**

GLENKINCHIE 1986, Distillers Edition, Double Matured, 43 vol

Finished in amontillado sherry.

COLOUR Full gold.

NOSE Lightly floral aroma of polished oak. Sweet lemon. Spices.

BODY Well-rounded.

PALATE The amontillado seems to heighten the interplay between sweetness
and dryness. First comes brown sugar and butter, then suddenly
dry nuttiness and surprising saltiness.

FINISH Sweet, astonishingly long, and soothing.

SCORE **79**

THE GLENLIVET

PRODUCER Chivas Brothers
REGION Highlands DISTRICT Speyside (Livet)
ADDRESS Ballindalloch, Banffshire, AB37 9DB
TEL 01340 821720 WEBSITE www.theglenlivet.com VC

THE GLITTERING PRIZE IN the great whisky takeover of 2001 was this distillery, in the most famous glen in Scotland: that of the small river Livet, which flows into the Spey. Among the distilling districts, the glen of the Livet is the one most deeply set into the mountains. Its water frequently flows underground for many miles. The mountain setting also provides the weather that whisky makers like. When distilling is in progress, the condensers work most effectively if cooled by very cold water, and in a climate to match. The malt whiskies made in the area are on the lighter side, very clean, flowery, subtle, and elegant.

The Livet's fame also has historical origins, in the period when different legislation and duties were applied to distilling in the Lowlands and Highlands. The Lowland distillers, nearer to the big cities, were treated as a legitimate industry; the more distant, thinly populated Highlands were perceived as having illegal distillers and smugglers in every glen. The glen of the Livet was a famous nest of illicit distillation. After legalization in 1824, the legendary spirit "from Glenlivet" was greatly in demand among merchants in the cities to the south.

Distillers absurdly far from the glen have used the geographical allusion, as if it were a synonym for Speyside in general, but this practice is now in decline as the greater interest in single malts focuses attention on the issue of origin. The distillery at the highest elevation in the glen (and perhaps in Scotland) is the one now known as Braeval. Until recently, it was known as Braes of Glenlivet, and it produces a honeyish, zesty whisky. Slightly lower is Tamnavulin, which has a notably light-bodied malt (though Tomintoul's, just across the hills in adjoining Avon valley, is lighter in palate). See entries for each.

Only one distillery in the area is permitted to call itself The Glenlivet. This is the distillery that was the first to become legal, and it now has an international reputation. The definite article is restricted even further in that it appears on only the official bottlings from the owning company of The Glenlivet distillery, Chivas. These carry the legend "Distilled by George & J. G. Smith" in small type at the bottom of the label, referring to the father and son who established the original business.

The Gaelic word "gobha", pronounced "gow" (as in typically Scottish names like McGowan) translates to Smith. It has been argued that the Gow family had supported Bonnie Prince Charlie and later found it politic to change their name to Smith, but this is open to question.

When the legalization of distillers was proposed by the Duke of Gordon, one of his tenants, George Smith, already an illicit whisky maker, was the first to apply for a licence. His son, John Gordon Smith, assisted and succeeded him. After distilling on two sites nearby, in 1858 the Smiths moved to the present location, Minmore, near the confluence of the Livet and Avon. The distillery stands at a point where the grassy valley is already beginning to steepen towards the mountains.

In 1880, the exclusive designation "The Glenlivet" was granted in a test case. The company remained independent until 1953, when it came under the same ownership as Glen Grant. In the 1960s, considerable quantities of the whisky were acquired by Gordon & MacPhail, leading to subsequent bottlings by them. These very old and sometimes vintage-dated versions are identified as George and J. G. Smith's Glenlivet Whisky.

The Glenlivet, Glen Grant, and Longmorn, and the blenders Chivas, were acquired by the North American and worldwide drinks group Seagram in 1977, since when the official bottlings have been energetically promoted.

By virtue of it being the biggest selling single malt in the large American market, The Glenlivet might be deemed commonplace, but it is a whisky of structure and complexity. It is distilled from water with a dash of hardness, and the peating of the malt is on the light side. About a third of the casks used have at some stage held sherry, though the proportion of first fill is considerably smaller than that.

HOUSE STYLE Flowery, fruity, peachy. Aperitif.

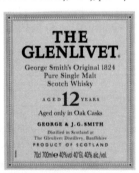

THE GLENLIVET 12-year-old, 40 vol

COLOUR Pale gold.

NOSE Remarkably flowery, clean and soft.

BODY Light to medium, firm, smooth.

PALATE Flowery, peachy, notes of vanilla, delicate balance.

FINISH Restrained, long, gently warming.

SCORE 85

THE GLENLIVET 12-year-old, French Oak Finish, 40 vol

COLOUR Warm gold to bronze.

NOSE Lots of flowery, fruity, fresh apple. Oak extract.

BODY Soft. Rounded.

PALATE Firm, rich rounded. Desert apples, blackcurrants, peaches, honey.

FINISH Crisp, clean oakiness.

SCORE 87

THE GLENLIVET 12-year-old, American Oak Finish, 40 vol

COLOUR Deep, refractive yellow.

NOSE The typically peachy bouquet seems to be accentuated.

BODY Firm. Medium to full. Very smooth.

PALATE Rich and fruity, with more peat smoke than usual. Cooked peaches.

FINISH Creamy tastes. Vanilla. Some burnt-grass bitterness.

SCORE 85

THE GLENLIVET 15-year-old, 43 vol

Mainly in duty-free/travel retail.

COLOUR Old gold.

NOSE Nutty, aromatic. Oak, dried apple/apple skin, freesia, hot sawdust.

BODY Light-bodied, good grip.

PALATE Clean and nutty with a floral lift.

FINISH Hint of smoke.

SCORE 80

THE GLENLIVET 18-year-old, 43 vol

COLOUR Deep gold to amber.

NOSE Elements beautifully combined. Depth of flowery aromas.
Very light touch of fresh peatiness. Some sweetness and a
hint of sherryish oak. Lightly appetizing.

BODY Firm, smooth.

PALATE Flowery and sweet at first, then developing peach-stone nuttiness.

FINISH Dry, appetizing. Very long, with interplay
of sweet and bitter flavours.

SCORE **87**

THE GLENLIVET Archive, 21-year-old, 43 vol

COLOUR Full gold to bronze.

NOSE Lively. Fruity. Peaty.

BODY Very firm and smooth.

PALATE Light, clean, cereal grain maltiness. Developing toastier, nuttier
flavours. Orange oil. Some macaroon-like sweetness, too.

FINISH Sweet grass. Smoky fragrance.

SCORE **85**

CELLAR NOTES

The first range of vintage-dated Glenlivets was drawn from batches distilled
in the early 1970s, and was released in the late 1990s. These were from years
with very limited stocks, which are now exhausted. The bottlings were
reviewed in the previous edition of this book, and are now hard to find.
They are collector's items. Special editions are now released under the rubric
The Cellar Collection.

GLENLOCHY

PRODUCER DCL/UDV
REGION Highlands DISTRICT Western Highlands
SITE OF FORMER DISTILLERY North Road, Fort William,
Inverness-shire, PH33 6TQ

THE LOCHY IS A RIVER that flows through the town of Fort William, at the foot of the mountain Ben Nevis. In addition to the Ben Nevis malt distillery, which is still very much in operation, Fort William for many years had another, called Glenlochy. This was built in 1898–1900, and changed little over the decades. It passed to DCL in 1953, lost its railway spur in the 1970s, and was closed in 1983. The very impressive pagoda still stands, and can be seen from the train. The equipment has gone, and the premises are now used as offices by unrelated businesses.

One sophisticated and geographically precise taster was reminded of Lebanese hashish by a Scotch Malt Whisky Society bottling of Glenlochy in the mid-1990s. The smokiness is less obvious in some recent bottlings, in which the wood seems tired but more oxidation and ester notes emerge. In 1995, United Distillers released a Rare Malts edition, with a similar bottling the following year.

HOUSE STYLE Peaty, fruity, creamy. With dessert or a book at bedtime.

GLENLOCHY 25-year-old, Distilled 1969, Bottled 1995, Rare Malts, 62.2 vol

COLOUR Old gold.

NOSE Charred oak and roasted chestnuts.

BODY Firm, smooth, oily.

PALATE Marron glacé and clotted cream.

FINISH Dry, big. Lemon zest and pepper.

SCORE **71**

GLENLOSSIE

PRODUCER Diageo
REGION Highlands DISTRICT Speyside (Lossie)
ADDRESS By Elgin, Morayshire, IV30 3SF
TEL 01343 862000

RESPECTED IN THE INDUSTRY (its whisky was once an important element in Haig blends), this distillery has a much lower profile among lovers of malts. A Flora and Fauna edition introduced in the early 1990s has made more connoisseurs aware of it, and there have since been bottlings from Signatory and Hart.

The distillery, in the valley of the Lossie, south of Elgin, was built in 1876, reconstructed 20 years later, and extended in 1962. Next door is the Mannochmore distillery, built in 1971.

HOUSE STYLE Flowery, clean, grassy, malty. Aperitif.

GLENLOSSIE 10-year-old, Flora and Fauna, 43 vol

COLOUR Fino sherry.

NOSE Fresh. Grass, heather, sandalwood.

BODY Light to medium. Soft, smooth.

PALATE Malty, dryish at first, then a range of sweeter, perfumy, spicy notes.

FINISH Spicy.

SCORE **76**

SOME INDEPENDENT BOTTLINGS:
Coopers Choice has bottled a 22-year-old at 43 vol. The nose is dry, oaty and biscuity with a rounded malty core; a direct rounded dram with a lightly chewy palate and a finish of dry grass. SCORE 75

GLENMORANGIE

PRODUCER Glenmorangie plc
REGION Highlands DISTRICT Northern Highlands
ADDRESS Tain, Ross-shire, IV19 1PZ
TEL 01862 892477 WEBSITE www.glenmorangie.com
EMAIL visitors@glenmorangieplc.co.uk VC

STILL THE BIGGEST SELLING MALT WHISKY in Scotland; still dividing opinion by its devotion to wood finishes (which offend some whisky conservatives); still, as a company, much respected and admired.

Glenmorangie pioneered "official" cask-strength bottlings at the beginning of the 1990s. In the middle of that decade, it began introducing wood finishes, from sherry variations such as fino to madeira, port, and French wines. More recently, it has introduced into some vattings of virgin American oak.

The company selects its own trees in the Ozark mountains of Missouri, has its wood seasoned by air drying (rather than kilning), and loans its casks for four years to the Jack Daniel's distillery in Lynchburg, Tennessee. A similar arrangement existed with Heaven Hill, in Bardstown, Kentucky, until the Bourbon distillery lost substantial amounts of wood in a fire. The wood policies at Glenmorangie are some of the most highly developed in the industry. It is significant that the man who developed them, Bill Lumsden, is styled Head of Distilleries and Maturation.

For all its achievements, Glenmorangie is one of the smaller companies in the industry. The distillery is near the pretty sandstone town of Tain (pop. 4000). The town and distillery are on the coast about 65 kilometres (40 miles) north of Inverness. From the A9 road, the short private drive passes between an assortment of trees and a dam shaped like a millpond. Beyond can be seen the waters of the Dornoch firth.

The distilling water rises on sandstone hills and flows over heather and clover, before emerging in a sandy pond about half a mile from the distillery. The sandstone surely contributes to the whisky's firmness of body, the flowers perhaps to its famously scenty character. (A French perfume house identified 26 aromas, from almond, bergamot, and cinnamon to verbena, vanilla, and wild mint. More recently, a New York fragrance company managed only 22).

HOUSE STYLE Creamy, leafy. Restorative or with dessert.
No obvious island character.

REGULAR BOTTLINGS, WITH AGE STATEMENTS

GLENMORANGIE 10-year-old, 40 vol

The principal version.

COLOUR Pale gold.

NOSE Spicy (cinnamon, walnut, sandalwood?), with some flowery sweetness. Fresh. A whiff of the sea. Enticing.

BODY On the light side of medium, but with some viscosity.

PALATE Spicy, flowery, and malty-sweet tones that are creamy, almost buttery. A suggestion of bananas?

FINISH Long and rounded.

SCORE 80

GLENMORANGIE 15-year-old, 43 vol

Finished in virgin oak.

COLOUR Deep gold.

NOSE Fresh sea air. More breezy.

BODY Smooth, slightly syrupy.

PALATE Lovely balance of sweet creaminess and herbal notes.

FINISH Appetizingly spicy. Clean hit of salt.

SCORE 81

GLENMORANGIE 18-year-old, 43 vol

COLOUR Full reddish amber.

NOSE Vanilla, mint, walnuts, sappy, oaky.

BODY Medium, smooth, fleshier.

PALATE Cookie-like and sweet at first, more walnuts, then the whole potpourri of spiciness.

FINISH Aromatic, nutty, lightly oaky.

SCORE 81

GLENMORANGIE 25-year-old, 43 vol

Mainly for the Asian/Pacific market.

COLOUR Dark polished oak.

NOSE An old shop, with fittings in polished oak, leather, and brass.

BODY Big. Slippery.

PALATE Cakey. Oily. Beeswax. A handsome whisky.

FINISH Late, gingery spiciness.

SCORE **80**

OTHER REGULARLY AVAILABLE EXPRESSIONS

GLENMORANGIE Cellar 13, 43 vol

Among the distillery's 14 cellars, this one is nearest to the sea.
The whiskies in this bottling are in the range of 10 to 12 years and more,
all matured in first-fill bourbon barrels.

COLOUR Primrose.

NOSE Soft, with fresh sandalwood, vanilla, and wild mint.

BODY Light to medium. Very smooth.

PALATE Notably soft and malty sweet, with butterscotch, vanilla, and honey.

FINISH Buttercups. Juicy, then late, emphatic saltiness. Very long indeed.

SCORE **81**

GLENMORANGIE Traditional, 100° proof, 57.2 vol

In the same style as the two above, but without chill filtering and at cask strength (in the
British version of the old proof system, 100° equalled 56.6–57.1 vol).

COLOUR Primrose, slightly oily.

NOSE Very aromatic and spicy.

BODY Smooth, firm, slightly gritty.

PALATE Richer, more substantial. Fuller flavours. Sandy-salty notes.

FINISH Robust. Intensely salty. Very long. Soothing.

SCORE **83**

GLENURY ROYAL

PRODUCER DCL
REGION Highlands   DISTRICT Eastern Highlands
SITE OF FORMER DISTILLERY Stonehaven, Kincardineshire, AB3 2PY

Has any valedictory bottling ever had the impact of Glenury's 50-year-old, issued as a special release in 2003? This voluptuous malt bore a recommended price tag of almost £1,000/$1,600 a bottle.

Glenury Royal was on the east coast, south of Aberdeen, and close to the fishing port of Stonehaven. The distillery's name derived from the glen that runs through the Ury district. The water for the whisky came from the Cowie, a river known for salmon and trout. The distillery was founded in 1825, partly to provide a market for barley in a period of agricultural depression. Founder Captain Robert Barclay was an athlete, known for an odd achievement: he was the first man to walk 1,000 miles in as many hours without a break. He was also a local Member of Parliament. Barclay had a friend at court to whom he referred coyly as "Mrs Windsor", and through whose influence he was given permission by King William IV to call his whisky "Royal". It was an excellent malt, judging from recent bottlings. The distillery was mothballed in 1985, and the site was later sold for a housing development.

HOUSE STYLE Aromatic, spicy, fruity. Book-at-bedtime.

GLENURY 1953, 50-year-old, 42.8 vol

COLOUR Dark orange.
NOSE Smoke. The burnt skin of chestnuts roasting.
BODY Rich, smooth, luxurious.
PALATE A whole box of liqueur chocolates concentrated into my tasting glass Dark chocolate, variously filled with coffee and cherry liqueurs Perhaps even peppermint.
FINISH Sappy, oaky dryness.

SCORE **89**

GLENURY ROYAL 21-year-old, Old Malt Cask, 50 vol

COLOUR Amber.

NOSE More wood on show. Soft and generous: hessian,
peanut skin, chocolate spread.

BODY Firm, dry.

PALATE Excellent concentration. Baked apple. Spicy oak. Complex.

FINISH Long and nutty.

SCORE 81

GLENURY-ROYAL 1972, Gordon & MacPhail, 40 vol

COLOUR Amber.

NOSE Mellow and mature. Honey and chestnut, plum, autumnal.
Hard toffee, black cherry.

BODY Long, elegant, and chewy.

PALATE The fruit sits heavily on the palate. Perfect balance. Coffee.

FINISH Long and attractive.

SCORE 84

GLENURY ROYAL 23-year-old, Distilled 1971,
Rare Malts, 61.3 vol

COLOUR Deep, reddish amber.

NOSE Peat, sherry, and polished oak.

BODY Medium, firm, smooth.

PALATE Smooth, tightly combined flavours, beautifully
rounded. Treacle toffee, nuts, cedary notes.

FINISH Very long. Starts oaky, then an explosion of long,
warming smokiness. A superb example of a Highland malt,
hitting as an oak-fisted heavyweight.

SCORE 80

GLENURY ROYAL 28-year-old, Distilled 1970, Rare Malts, 58.4 vol

COLOUR Shining gold.

NOSE Nutty, almondy, oloroso sherry.

BODY Very firm, rounded. Less sherryish muscle, more of an
elegant middleweight.

PALATE Honey, lemons, pistachio nuts, angelica, garden mint.

FINISH Like biting into a green leaf. Tree-bark woodiness.
Cinnamon. Fragrant. Long.

SCORE 79

HIGHLAND PARK

PRODUCER The Edrington Group
REGION Highlands ISLAND Orkney
ADDRESS Kirkwall, Orkney, KW15 1SU TEL 01856 874619 VC
WEBSITE www.highlandpark.co.uk

THIS GREAT ORCADIAN DISTILLERY is now the only islander in The Edrington Group, with the sale of Bunnahabhain, on Islay. Presumably the idea was to concentrate on Highland Park as the group's island malt, and pitch the distinctiveness of Orkney against fashionable Islay. Devotees might expect a clamour of new bottlings from Highland Park: labelled to emphasize the distinctly young, heathery nature of Orkney's peat; the simple beauty of the maltings at the distillery; the big, bulbous stills; the winds that blow salt on to the shore. So far, nothing much has happened, but no doubt it will.

Highland Park is the greatest all-rounder in the world of malt whisky. It is definitely in an island style, but combining all the elements of a classic single malt: smokiness (with its own heather-honey accent), maltiness, smoothness, roundness, fullness of flavour, and length of finish.

Subject to ambitious plans for the Shetland islands, Highland Park is the northernmost of Scotland's distilleries. It dates from at least 1798.

HOUSE STYLE Smoky and full-flavoured. At 18 or 25 years old, with dessert or a cigar. The yet older vintages with a book at bedtime.

HIGHLAND PARK 12-year-old, 40 vol

COLOUR Amber.

NOSE Smoky, "garden bonfire" sweetness, heathery, malty, hint of sherry.

BODY Medium, exceptionally smooth.

PALATE Succulent, with smoky dryness, heather-honey
sweetness, and maltiness.

FINISH Teasing, heathery, delicious.

SCORE 90

HIGHLAND PARK 15-year-old, 40 vol

COLOUR Amber.

NOSE Thick and sweet. Botrytis. Squashed apricot, over-ripe pear.
Toasted almond, beech nut.

BODY Chewy.

PALATE Great balance between caramelized fruit, honey, and heathery
smoke. Mouth-filling. Fudge. Malt.

FINISH Treacle toffee.

SCORE 87

HIGHLAND PARK 18-year-old, 43 vol

COLOUR Refractive, pale gold.

NOSE Warm, notably flowery. Heather honey, fresh oak, sap, peat,
smoky fragrance. Very aromatic and appetizing.

BODY Remarkably smooth, firm, rounded.

PALATE Lightly salty. Leafy (vine leaves?), pine nuts. Lots of flavour
development: nuts, honey, cinnamon, dryish ginger.

FINISH Spicy, very dry, oaky, smoky, hot.

SCORE 92

INCHGOWER

PRODUCER Diageo
REGION Highlands DISTRICT Speyside
ADDRESS Buckie, Banffshire, AB56 2AB TEL 01542 836700

Tastes more like a coastal malt than a Speysider. It is both, the distillery being on the coast near the fishing town of Buckie, but not far from the mouth of the river Spey. To the palate expecting a more flowery, elegant Speyside style, this can seem assertive, or even astringent, in its saltiness. With familiarity, that can become addictive. The Inchgower distillery was built in 1871, and expanded in 1966. Its whisky is an important element in the Bell's blend.

HOUSE STYLE Dry, salty. Restorative or aperitif.

INCHGOWER 14-year-old, Flora and Fauna, 43 vol

COLOUR Pale gold.

NOSE An almost chocolatey spiciness, then sweet notes like edible seaweed, and finally a whiff of saltier sea character. Overall, dry and complex.

BODY Light to medium. Smooth.

PALATE Starts sweet and malty, with lots of flavour developing, eventually becoming drier and salty.

FINISH Very salty, lingering appetizingly on the tongue.

SCORE 76

OTHER VERSIONS OF INCHGOWER

A Rare Malts 1974, at cask strength, had sea air in the nose; salted cashew, and edible-seaweed flavours. SCORE 79. A 19-year-old from Cadenhead , at 46 vol, is chocolatey, nutty (roast chestnuts), smoke, oak, and resin. SCORE 78.

JURA

PRODUCER Whyte and Mackay Ltd
REGION Highlands ISLAND Jura
ADDRESS Craighouse, Jura, Argyll, PA60 7XT
TEL 01496 820240 WEBSITE www.isleofjura.com VC

EVERY VISITOR TO ISLAY also makes the crossing to Jura. The two are so close that they tend to be seen as one. While Islay has seven working distilleries, Jura has just the one. While Islay has some very assertive whiskies, Jura's is delicate – but gains power with age. Under new ownership, the distillery has been more active in introducing new products and marketing them with some vigour.

Two extraordinarily young bottlings, at three and four years old, were made for the Japanese market. Both showed considerable potential. The younger was clean, malty, and assertive, with good maritime flavours. The marginally less young version was more earthy, flowery, and fruity. In the British market, "Superstition" is a sweeter, richer, mature whisky, but seems a little confected, like its marketing story.

The first distillery on the site seems to have been founded around 1810, and rebuilt in 1876. Although a couple of buildings dating back to its early days are still in use, the present distillery was built during the late 1950s and early 1960s, and enlarged in the 1970s.

The name Jura derives from the Norse word for deer. These outnumber people, on an island 55 by 11 kilometres (34 by 7 miles). Jura has about 225 human inhabitants, among whom its most famous was George Orwell. He went there to find a healthy, peaceful place in which to write the novel *1984*. There is a whisky named after him in the Jura range.

HOUSE STYLE Piney, lightly oily, soft, salty. Aperitif.

ISLE OF JURA Superstition, No Age Statement, 45 vol

COLOUR Bronze satin.

NOSE Very light peat smoke, but also some sherryish sweetness. Sweet hay.

BODY Smooth. Waxy.

PALATE Piney, honeyish. Developing sweet creaminess. Opens very slowly.

FINISH Salty, with a surprising sting.

 SCORE **80**

ISLE OF JURA 10-year-old, 40 vol

COLOUR Bright gold.

NOSE Oily, lightly piney, earthy, salty, dry.

BODY Light, slightly oily, soft.

PALATE Sweetish; slowly developing a slight island dryness and saltiness.

FINISH A little malty sweetness and some saltiness.

 SCORE **72**

ISLE OF JURA Legacy 10-year-old, 40 vol

The vatting for this version additionally contains substantially older malts.

COLOUR Amber.

NOSE Nutty and malty with a slight metallic note.
Turf and flour sacks, rising dough.

PALATE Firm, sweet bracken. Fresh and clean. Lunchtime.

FINISH Squeeze of fruit juice, then malt.

 SCORE **70**

ISLE OF JURA, 16-year-old, 40 vol

COLOUR Full gold to bronze.

NOSE Freshly chopped pine trees. Ferns. Forest floor.

BODY Light, firm, oily-creamy. Dryish.

PALATE Ground coriander. Orange. Rhubarb jam. Buttered scones.

FINISH Salty.

SCORE **77**

ISLE OF JURA Orwell, 42 vol

COLOUR Gold.

NOSE Quite woody and prickly to start. Heather moor, marine. Mossy.

BODY Dry.

PALATE Broad with light smoke all the way playing against central
tangerine-flavoured sweetness. Some complexity.

FINISH Nutty.

 SCORE **78**

KNOCKANDO

PRODUCER Diageo
REGION Highlands DISTRICT Speyside
ADDRESS Knockando, Aberlour, Banffshire, AB38 7RT
TEL 01340 882000

M ORE WAS HEARD OF this elegant whisky – in Britain, at least – when it was the most promoted malt in the portfolio of IDV, before the merger that created Diageo in 1997.

Knockando is among a small group of malts that are especially influential in the J&B (Justerini & Brooks) blends (*see* Glen Spey, The Singleton/Auchroisk, *and* Strathmill). Knockando is a sophisticated malt, and its labelling policy is somewhat elaborate. In the US, where some consumers believe the guarantee "12-year-old" essential to identify a premium malt, this phrase is used, along with the year of distillation, on the label of the principal version. In Britain, the malt is marketed under its season of distillation. The notion is that the malt is bottled when it is mature, rather than at a specific age.

One season does not differ dramatically from another, though there are very subtle differences. At older ages, the whisky gains greatly in complexity and sherry character.

The water with which the whisky is made rises from granite and flows over peat. The distillery's name, pronounced "knock-AN-do" (or 'du) sounds allusively comical to English speakers, but translates perfectly sensibly as "a little black hill". Knockando is hidden in a fold in the hills overlooking the river Spey at a fine spot for salmon fishing. The distillery was established in 1898.

HOUSE STYLE Elegant, with suggestions of berry fruits. Aperitif.

KNOCKANDO 1989, 43 vol

COLOUR Bright gold.

NOSE Faint, grassy, sweetish, peat. Lemon grass. Marshmallow. Shortbread.

BODY Light but smooth.

PALATE Soft. Creamy. Faintly honeyed. Raspberries. Lemon zest.

FINISH Nutty, toffeeish dryness. Gently appetizing.

 SCORE 76

KNOCKANDO 18-year-old, 1980, 43 vol

Available mainly in the US.

COLOUR Medium gold.

NOSE More shortbread. Almonds. Nice balance of late lemon.

BODY Creamier. Rounder. Very smooth indeed.

PALATE Nuttier, spicier, drier. Tightly combined flavours.

FINISH Late fruit, lemon grass, and light peat. Very appetizing.

 SCORE 78

KNOCKANDO Slow Matured, Distilled 1980, Bottled 1998, 43 vol

Available mainly in France.

COLOUR Bright, medium gold.

NOSE Seems faintly peatier than the version above.

BODY Fractionally oilier?

PALATE Possibly more lemon and raspberry fruitiness.

FINISH Crisp. Shortbread. Late warmth.

SCORE 78

LAGAVULIN

PRODUCER Diageo
REGION Islay DISTRICT South Shore
ADDRESS Port Ellen, Islay, Argyll, PA42 7DZ TEL 01496 302730
WEBSITE www.discovering-distilleries.com/www.malts.com

RECENT SHORTAGES OF LAGAVULIN date back to a period 16 years ago when the distillery was closed for some time for repairs and renewal. In those days, Lagavulin worked only two days a week. Today, it cannot produce enough to meet anticipated demand. Until the shortage, it was the best selling Islay malt, having overtaken its neighbour Laphroaig. Consideration has been given to adding a pair of stills, but it is felt that might "damage the integrity" of the beautifully kept distillery.

Lagavulin has the driest and most sustained attack of any readily available whisky, though in recent years it has seemed less brutal than it once was.

The launch in 1997–98 of a version identified as being finished in Pedro Ximénez sherry casks excited great interest. How would this famously robust whisky live with the most hefty of sherries? Would each cancel out the other, so that the punch was finally restrained? Or would the two combine to produce a superpower? Neither is quite the case. The two elements are like heavyweights punching in a clinch.

The distillery's water arrives by way of a fast-flowing stream that no doubt picks up plenty of peat on the way there. The maturation warehouses are battered by the sea, and they have their own jetty.

Lagavulin (pronounced "lagga-voolin") means "the hollow where the mill is". There are reputed to have been ten illicit stills on this bay in the mid-1700s. Lagavulin traces its history to 1816.

HOUSE STYLE Dry, smoky, complex. Restorative or nightcap.

LAGAVULIN 12-year-old, Cask Strength, Special Release 2003, 57.8 vol

COLOUR Unusually pale. Vinho verde.

NOSE Delightfully gentle smokiness, but very restrained for Lagavulin. Some floweriness.

BODY Very light.

PALATE Marshmallow. Digestive biscuits. Assam tea.

FINISH Smoky. Some of the peatiness that might be expected in Lagavulin. Slightly fruity. Warming. Firm. Long.

SCORE 91

LAGAVULIN 16-year-old, 43 vol

COLOUR Full amber.

NOSE Sea spray, peat smoke. Stings the back of the nose.

BODY Full, smooth, very firm.

PALATE Peaty dryness like gunpowder tea. As the palate develops, oily, grassy, and, in particular, salty notes emerge.

FINISH Peat fire. Warming. A bear hug.

SCORE 95

LAGAVULIN 1979, Double Matured, Distillers Edition, 43 vol

Finished in Pedro Ximénez sherry casks.

COLOUR Orange sandstone.

NOSE Fresh attack, with hits of peat, tar, sulphur, and salt, soothed with beeswax.

BODY Full. Syrupy.

PALATE Rich and extremely sweet, then smoky, becoming medicinal, and eventually seaweedy.

FINISH Pepper, salt, sand. What it loses in distillery character, it gains in a different dimension of distinctiveness.

SCORE 95

LAGAVULIN 1979, Murray McDavid Mission Range, 46 vol

COLOUR Pale straw.

NOSE Phenolic. Smoked fish. Hot stones on the beach. Bog myrtle.

BODY Soft.

PALATE Fragrant smoke all the way. Soot. Sweet spot in the centre keeps it balanced.

FINISH Enveloping smoke.

SCORE 88

LINKWOOD

PRODUCER Diageo
REGION Highlands ISLAND Speyside (Lossie)
ADDRESS Elgin, Morayshire, IV30 3RD TEL 01343 862000

A SECRET NATURE RESERVE or a distillery? Linkwood's appropriately flowery Speyside whisky is increasingly appreciated, judging from the profusion of independent bottlings.

The dam that provides the cooling water is a port of call to tufted ducks and goldeneyes – and a seasonal home to wagtails, oyster catchers, mute swans, and otters. In the 4 hectares (10 acres) of the site, nettles attract red admiral and small tortoiseshell butterflies; cuckoo flowers entice the orange tip variety; bluebells seduce bees.

The distillery was founded in 1821. The older of its two still-houses, in the original buildings, continues to be used for a few months each year. It produces a slightly heavier spirit than the larger still-house built in the 1960s and extended in the 1970s.

HOUSE STYLE Floral. Rose-water? Cherries? Delicious with a slice of fruitcake.

LINKWOOD 12-year-old, Flora and Fauna, 43 vol

COLOUR Full primrose.

NOSE Remarkably flowery and petal-like. Buttercups. Grass. Fragrant.

BODY Medium, rounded, slightly syrupy.

PALATE Starts slowly, and has a long, sustained development to marzipan, roses, and fresh sweetness. One to savour.

FINISH Perfumy, dryish. Lemon zest.

SCORE **82**

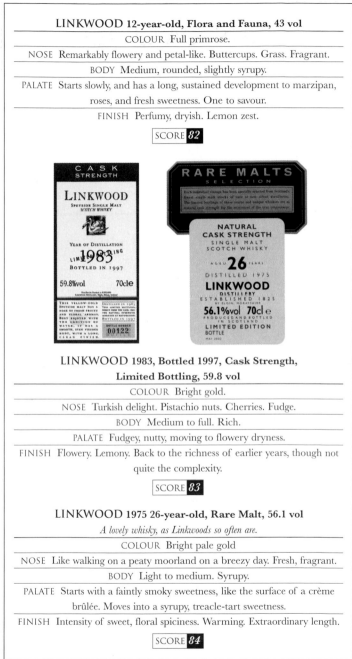

LINKWOOD 1983, Bottled 1997, Cask Strength, Limited Bottling, 59.8 vol

COLOUR Bright gold.

NOSE Turkish delight. Pistachio nuts. Cherries. Fudge.

BODY Medium to full. Rich.

PALATE Fudgey, nutty, moving to flowery dryness.

FINISH Flowery. Lemony. Back to the richness of earlier years, though not quite the complexity.

SCORE **83**

LINKWOOD 1975 26-year-old, Rare Malt, 56.1 vol

A lovely whisky, as Linkwoods so often are.

COLOUR Bright pale gold

NOSE Like walking on a peaty moorland on a breezy day. Fresh, fragrant.

BODY Light to medium. Syrupy.

PALATE Starts with a faintly smoky sweetness, like the surface of a crème brûlée. Moves into a syrupy, treacle-tart sweetness.

FINISH Intensity of sweet, floral spiciness. Warming. Extraordinary length.

SCORE **84**

LOCHNAGAR

PRODUCER Diageo
REGION Highlands   DISTRICT Eastern Highlands
ADDRESS Crathie, Ballater, Aberdeenshire, AB35 5TB
TEL 01339 742705
WEBSITE www.discovering-distilleries.com/www.malts.com   VC

QUEEN VICTORIA'S FAVOURITE DISTILLERY was once on the tourist route, but has recently been used by Diageo as a place in which to educate its own staff and customers on the subject of malt whisky. The process of making whisky can best be understood in a small, traditional distillery, and Lochnagar qualifies on both counts. It is Diageo's smallest. It is also very pretty – and makes delicious whisky.

The distillery is at the foot of the mountain of Lochnagar, near the river Dee, not far from Aberdeen. A man believed originally to have been an illicit whisky maker established the first legal Lochnagar distillery in 1826, and the present premises were built in 1845. Three years later, the royal family acquired nearby Balmoral as their Scottish country home. The then owner, John Begg, wrote a note inviting Prince Albert to visit. The Prince and Queen Victoria arrived the very next day. Soon afterwards, the distillery began to supply the Queen, and became known as Royal Lochnagar. Her Majesty is said to have laced her claret with the whisky, perhaps anticipating wood finishes. There is no claret finish at Lochnagar as yet. The 12-year-old is aged in second-fill casks, while the Selected Reserve has 50 per cent sherry.

HOUSE STYLE Malty, fruity, spicy, cake-like. After dinner.

ROYAL LOCHNAGAR 12-year-old, 40 vol

COLOUR Full gold.

NOSE Big, with some smokiness.

BODY Medium to full. Smooth.

PALATE Light smokiness, restrained fruitiness, and malty sweetness.

FINISH Again, dry smokiness and malty sweetness. The first impression
is of dryness, then comes the sweet, malty counterpoint.

SCORE **80**

ROYAL LOCHNAGAR Selected Reserve,
No Age Statement, 43 vol

COLOUR Amber red.

NOSE Very sherryish indeed. Spices, ginger cake.

BODY Big, smooth.

PALATE Lots of sherry, malty sweetness, spiced bread, ginger cake.
Obviously contains some very well matured whisky.

FINISH Smoky.

SCORE **83**

ROYAL LOCHNAGAR 23-year-old, Rare Malts,
Distilled 1973, 59.7 vol

COLOUR Bright gold.

NOSE Sweet, syrupy, parkin-like.

BODY Medium. Very soft.

PALATE Very appetizing, fresh, clean sweetness.
Very good flavour development.

FINISH Marzipan and nutty dryness.

SCORE **81**

ROYAL LOCHNAGAR Rare Malts, 24-year-old,
Distilled 1972, 55.7 vol

COLOUR Full, bright gold.

NOSE Fresh soda bread. Yeasty.

BODY Light to medium. Smooth.

PALATE Appetizing, spicy ginger cake.
Lots of flavour development and complexity.

FINISH Cake dusted with cinnamon, nutmeg.
Satisfying. Very long indeed.

SCORE **81**

THE MACALLAN

PRODUCER The Edrington Group
REGION Highlands DISTRICT Speyside
ADDRESS Aberlour, Banffshire, AB38 9RX
TEL 01340 872280 WEBSITE www.themacallan.com VC

A S BRONZED AND MUSCULAR as a practitioner of the noble art, Macallan is Speyside's best known heavyweight – and constantly embracing a new challenge. In one such engagement, Macallan has over the years collected, and bought at auction, bottles of its own whisky from the 1800s.

An 1874 Macallan, bought by the company for £4000/$6000, inspired a bold attempt to replicate its character by making a vatting from stocks. The key seemed to be an accent toward fino sherry wood, rather than the dry oloroso currently preferred. There was sufficient fino wood in Macallan's warehouses, and a credible replica of the 1874 was produced. This appeared at the time to be a unique exercise, but a further three replica whiskies have been created since.

It is not necessary to make replicas of Macallans from the early to mid-1900s, as sufficient casks were laid down. Some of these whiskies, designated by the company as Exceptional Single Casks, have been released, one at a time, in recent years.

From the 1920s, it seemed to have become pricey to lay down generous quantities. Most of the whisky was still in cask, but some had been bottled, to prevent evaporation taking it below the minimum legal strength. One hogshead yielded only 40 bottles; the most generous butt provided 548.

It was decided to create an offering of very old whiskies. What constitutes "very old"? The definition was set at more than 30 years old, i.e. distilled no later than 1972. Not all years were represented in the warehouses, but the chronology was surprisingly thorough. Master distiller David Robertson and whisky maker Bob Dalgarno nosed nearly 600 casks, selecting one or two from each year for vintage bottlings. Where there was no stock for a year, Macallan bought back casks, and even cases of bottles, from the trade and collectors. The range launched in 2003, has the rubric "Fine and Rare", with its own style of bottles, and labels highlighting vintage dates. This packaging was also applied to bottles drawn from stock, or bought back; they were all rebottled. All of the whiskies were hand bottled at the distillery, at cask strength. Prices range from £20,000/$33,000 for the most expensive bottle to £65/$110 for the cheapest miniature. The initial offering amounts to 10,000 bottles, valued at just under £14 million/$23 million. The whiskies can be bought, or a catalogue obtained, from specialist retailers; through Macallan's website or at the distillery gift shop. There are even some bars selling these whiskies, inevitably at very high prices.

"Rather than dribbling out occasional vintages, we wanted to make a full range available," explained David Robertson. "If someone is celebrating an important birthday, for example, they might like a gift of whisky from the year they were born. Most distilleries don't have the breadth of stock to do this. We can."

To collectors, no name has the magic of Macallan. The name derives from the Macallan church, now a ruin, on the Easter Elchies estate, which is on a cliff overlooking Telford's bridge over the Spey, at Craigellachie. Immediately across the river is Aberlour.

A farmer on the hillside is believed to have made whisky from his own barley in the 1700s. Macallan became a legal distillery as soon as that was possible, in 1824. In 1998, the estate farm was put back into service to grow Golden Promise barley, albeit a token amount in relation to Macallan's requirements. The manor house from the early days has been restored as a venue for the entertaining of visitors.

Macallan has long been a renowned contributor to blends, notably including The Famous Grouse. In 1968–69, the company decided that single malts would also be an important element of the future.

The character of Macallan has traditionally begun with Golden Promise barley, but this Scottish variety is becoming hard to find. Cultivation has drastically diminished because Golden Promise offers a relatively ungenerous yield of grain to farmers. Its yield to distillers in terms of spirit is also on the low side, but the nutty, oily, silky flavours produced are delicious. Until about 1994, Macallan used only Golden Promise. Since then, there has been the odd year when a good harvest and reduced production of whisky has made this possible, but at other times its share of the grist has dropped to 30 or 25 per cent, and even approached 20. More common varieties such as Chariot or Optic have provided the greater share.

Some distillers do not concern themselves with barley varieties, but simply set out a technical specification of performance. Many take the same view of yeasts, and in recent years some have switched from using two strains to one. These arguments seem to ignore a fundamental point: what the consumer gets out of the glass must depend upon what the producer puts in. Macallan has in recent years used four yeasts, and currently employs two of them. The company believes that this particular combination enhances its fruity, spicy aromas and flavours.

Macallan's oily, creamy richness is enhanced by the use of especially small stills. When the company has expanded output to cope with demand, it has added more stills, rather than building bigger ones. The number grew from six to 21 between 1965 and 1975. The wash stills are heated by gas burners. This use of direct flame can impart a caramelization of the malt which steam heat does not. Macallan also believes it takes the narrowest cut in the industry.

When Macallan decided to market a single malt, the principals made tastings from stock and decided that their whisky tasted best from dry oloroso butts.

Meanwhile, faced with the high cost of obtaining the casks, Macallan has been carrying out exhaustive research to establish exactly what are the influences on flavour. Given that an oak tree takes 100 years to reach maturity, and the whisky another ten or a dozen, progress is slow.

The European oak variety *Quercus robur* is rich in tannins, and imparts both the full colour and the resiny, spicy (clove, cinnamon, nutmeg) fragrances and flavours that are typical of Macallan.

Macallan's current view is that the reaction between wood and sherry is also of great importance. This appears to wash out the harshest tannins and help release a rich, rounded spiciness. This is felt to be far more significant than any aromas and flavours imparted by the sherry itself. One rather extreme piece of research suggested that barely a third of aromas and flavours originated from the spirit, almost 60 per cent from the oak, and less than 10 per cent from the sherry.

The current regime is that the butts are first filled with mosto (grape juice) for three months' primary fermentation. They then have two years with maturing sherry in a bodega. They are then shipped to Scotland. Between 70 and 80 per cent of Macallan is matured in first-fill butts, the remainder in second-fill. In the principal versions of The Macallan first and second fill is vatted in broadly those proportions.

HOUSE STYLE Big, oaky, resiny sherried, flowery-fruity. Spicy. Very long. After dinner.

THE MACALLAN Distiller's Choice, No Age Statement, 40 vol

Mainly for the Japanese market.

COLOUR Bronze. Paler than most Macallans.

NOSE Especially fragrant.

BODY Medium. Very smooth.

PALATE Lightly buttery and malty. Lively, youthful flavours.
Emphasis on classic Speyside floweriness rather than sherry.

FINISH Highlights the crisp dryness of Macallan.

SCORE *81*

THE MACALLAN 10-year-old, 40 vol

Mainly for the UK market.

COLOUR Amber.

NOSE Sherry. Butterscotch. Honeyish malt character.
Depth of aromas even at this young age.

BODY Full, without being syrupy.

PALATE Lots of sherry, without being rich. Plenty of malt.
Sweetish. Rounded.

FINISH Satisfying, malty, gingery, becoming dry, with a hint of smoke.

SCORE *87*

THE MACALLAN 12-year-old, 43 vol

Mainly for export markets.

COLOUR Amber.

NOSE Sherry, honey, flowery notes.

BODY Full, smooth.

PALATE The first hints of flowering currant. Altogether more expressive.

FINISH Slightly more rounded.

SCORE *91*

THE MACALLAN 15-year-old, 43 vol

Now hard to find.

COLOUR Medium amber.

NOSE This age best expresses the estery fruitiness of Macallan.

BODY Full, very smooth.

PALATE Toffeeish. Gently fruity and spicy.
Hints of peat. A little lacking in dimension.

FINISH Grassy. Lightly peaty.

SCORE **92**

THE MACALLAN 25-year-old, 43 vol

COLOUR Full amber red.

NOSE At this age, a definite smokiness manifests itself, and
embraces all the other aromas that have appeared earlier.

BODY Full, firm, round.

PALATE The smokiness greatly enhances the complexity.

FINISH Dry, complex, very long.

SCORE **95**

THE MACALLAN 30-year-old, 43 vol

COLOUR Full orange.

NOSE This age best highlights the resiny contributions of the oak itself.
Reminiscent of polished oak. The faintly piney, floral aromas of
furniture polish. The waxed skin of fresh tangerines. Orange zest.

BODY Medium to full.

PALATE Despite its great age, no aggressive oakiness or overbearing
sherry. Tightly combined flavours. Its great appeal is its mellow
maturity. Complex. Just a whiff of smoke.

FINISH Dry, warming, soothing, but disappears too quickly.

SCORE **95**

MACALLAN 18-YEAR-OLDS

Most years, The Macallan has released an 18-year-old, at 43 vol, in which
some malt lovers find the most robust interplay of the estery whisky and the
dry oloroso maturation. These are vatted to offer continuity of character, but
inevitably they vary slightly. The following five bottlings at 18 years old are
each given their own score. This is a new feature in the fifth edition of this
book. In the fourth edition, when this year-by-year review of the
18-year-olds was introduced, an overall score of 94 was given for the category.

1984 Attractive, deep tawny colour. Appetizing, yet rich, oaky, raisiny
aroma. Slippery body. Flavours establish a grip nonetheless, and
pace themselves. Perfumy notes. Chocolate fudge. Malty middle.
Clean, crisp, gingery spiciness in finish. SCORE 94

1983 Fractionally darker and more reddish. More sappy aroma.
More immediately gingery and spicy. Drier. More resiny.
Harder edge. Arguably harsher, more robust. SCORE 93

1982 Deep, dark orange. Fruity, toffeeish aroma. Sweetish.
More toffee and chocolate in palate. Beeswax. Leafy. Cilantro?
Chilli-pepper finish. SCORE 94

1981 Bright, deep amber. Palest colour in this flight. Aromas and
flavours so melded as to be hard to unpick. Smooth, urbane. Like a
person who answers questions with dismissive brevity to imply a loftier
knowledge. The whisky eventually admits to some spiciness and a
pleasantly oaky dryness in the finish. SCORE 93

1980 Deep bronze. Fullest colour in this flight. Perfumy, spicy aroma, with
cinnamon accent. Oily. Smooth. Toffeeish. Becoming spicy. SCORE 92

MILLBURN

PRODUCER DCL
REGION Highlands DISTRICT Speyside (Inverness)
SITE OF FORMER DISTILLERY Millburn Road, Inverness,
Inverness-shire, IV2 3QX

A S THE TRAIN FROM LONDON finishes its 11-hour journey to Inverness, it glides by recognizable distillery buildings that are now a pub-steakhouse. At least there is still drink on the premises.

Millburn is believed to have dated from 1807, and its buildings from 1876 and 1922. It was owned for a time by Haig's. The distillery closed in 1985. Whiskies distilled a decade earlier have been released at 18 years and now 25, as Rare Malts.

HOUSE STYLE Smoky, aromatic. Night cap.

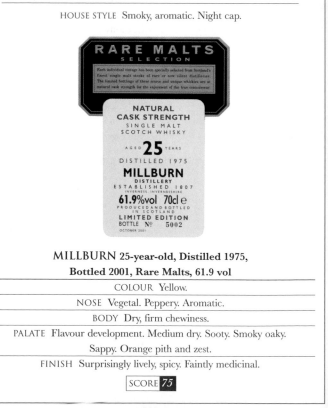

MILLBURN 25-year-old, Distilled 1975,
Bottled 2001, Rare Malts, 61.9 vol

COLOUR Yellow.
NOSE Vegetal. Peppery. Aromatic.
BODY Dry, firm chewiness.
PALATE Flavour development. Medium dry. Sooty. Smoky oaky. Sappy. Orange pith and zest.
FINISH Surprisingly lively, spicy. Faintly medicinal.

SCORE 75

MORTLACH

PRODUCER Diageo
REGION Highlands   DISTRICT Speyside (Dufftown)
ADDRESS Dufftown, Banffshire, AB55 4AQ
TEL 01340 822100   WEBSITE www.malts.com

ALL THE PLEASURES OF A GOOD SPEYSIDE single malt are found in Mortlach: floweriness, peatiness, smokiness, maltiness, and fruitiness. Its complexity may well arise from its extraordinary miscellany of stills. In the course of a history stretching from the earliest days of legal distilling, successive managers seem to have been heretics: fiddling with the shape, size, and design of stills to achieve the result they desired. It seems that they strayed so far from the orthodoxies of the industry that they were never corralled, and the whisky was so good that no one wanted to risk changing it. Nor does anyone wholly understand how the combination of stills achieves its particular result. The whisky has such individuality that its character is not overwhelmed by sherry maturation. While UDV/Diageo has over the years moved away from sherry, and argued for "distillery character", Mortlach has not been bound by that orthodoxy, either.

HOUSE STYLE A Speyside classic: elegant and flowery yet supple and muscular. Immensely complex, with great length. After dinner or bedtime.

SPEYSIDE
SINGLE MALT
SCOTCH WHISKY

MORTLACH

was the first of seven
distilleries in *Dufftown*. In the
19th farm animals kept in
adjoining byres were fed on
barley left over from processing.
Today *water* from springs in
the *CONVAL HILLS* is used to
produce this delightful
smooth, fruity single
MALT SCOTCH WHISKY.

AGED 16 YEARS

Distilled & Bottled in SCOTLAND
MORTLACH DISTILLERY
Dufftown, Keith, Banffshire, Scotland

43% vol   70 cl

MORTLACH 16-year-old, Flora and Fauna, 43 vol

COLOUR Profound, rich amber.

NOSE Dry oloroso sherry. Smoky, peaty.

BODY Medium to full, firm, smooth.

PALATE Sherryish, smoky, peaty, sappy, some fruitiness, assertive.

FINISH Long and dry.

SCORE *81*

MORTLACH 1980, Bottled 1997,
Cask Strength Limited Bottling, 63.1 vol

COLOUR Very attractive. Bright, orangey amber.

NOSE Distinct peat character. Stalky. Lime skins.

BODY Big, rich.

PALATE Flowery. Buttercups. Syrupy. Rich sherry notes. Very big in
the middle, with lots of flavour development. Soft mint humbugs.

FINISH More mint, becoming drier. An outstanding digestif.

SCORE *85*

MORTLACH 22-year-old, Distilled 1972, Rare Malts, 65.3 vol

COLOUR Very full gold.

NOSE Cereal grains. Fresh baked bread. Some smoky peat.

BODY Remarkably smooth, layered.

PALATE Hugely nutty. Developing from dryness to sweeter
juiciness. Then sweet smokiness.

FINISH Complex, with barley-sugar nuttiness and surging warmth.
Tremendous length.

SCORE *85*

NORTH PORT

PRODUCER DCL/UDV
REGION Highlands DISTRICT Eastern Highlands
SITE OF FORMER DISTILLERY Brechin, Angus, DD9 6BE

THE NAME INDICATES THE NORTH GATE of the small, once-walled city of Brechin. The distillery was built in 1820. The pioneering whisky writer, Alfred Barnard, who toured Scotland's distilleries in the 1880s, recorded that this one obtained its barley from the farmers around Brechin, and its peat and water from the Grampian mountains. The present-day writer, Derek Cooper, reports that the condensers were cooled in a stream that ran through the distillery. North Port was modernized in the 1970s, and closed in 1983. It has now been sold for redevelopment.

HOUSE STYLE Dry, fruity, gin-like. Aperitif.

NORTH PORT 19-year-old, Distilled 1979,
Bottled 1998, Rare Malts, 61 vol

COLOUR Bright, pale gold.
NOSE Dry, lightly smoky, grassy. Dry fruitiness.
BODY Light to medium. Some viscosity.
PALATE Light. Leafy. Dried apricot. Dried banana. Toasted marshmallow.
FINISH Dry, spirity, sharp. Cedary.

SCORE **68**

OBAN

PRODUCER Diageo
REGION Highlands   DISTRICT Western Highlands
ADDRESS Stafford Street, Oban, Argyll, PA34 5NH
TEL 01631 572004
WEBSITE www.discovering-distilleries.com/www.malts.com   VC

ENTHUSIASTS FOR THE WESTERN HIGHLAND malts sometimes dismiss Oban as being too restrained. With the 14-year-old augmented not only by the Montilla fino, but also by a 2002 Limited Release, there is now enough of an oeuvre to prove otherwise.

Oban is one of the few Western Highland distilleries on the mainland. It is a small distillery in a small town, but within that scale has a commanding position. Oban is regarded as the capital of the Western Highlands, and the distillery has a central site on the main street, facing the sea.

The principal expression of its whisky, the 14-year-old, has a label design incorporating a summary of the town's history: settled by Mesolithic cave dwellers before 5000BC; later by Celts, Picts, and Vikings. It was a fishing village, and in the era of railways and steamships became a gateway to the islands of the west, which it still is. Travellers following the muses of Mendelssohn, Turner, Keats, or Wordsworth to Mull or Iona, or Fingal's Cave, return to see a harbourfront centred on the distillery – backed by mossy, peaty hills whence its water flows.

A family of merchants in the town became brewers and distillers in 1794, though the present buildings probably date from the 1880s. The still-house was rebuilt in the late 1960s and early 1970s.

HOUSE STYLE Medium, with fresh peat and a whiff of the sea.
With seafood or game, or after dinner.

OBAN 14-year-old, 43 vol

COLOUR Full gold to amber.

NOSE "Pebbles on the beach", said one taster. A whiff of the sea,
but also a touch of fresh peat, and some maltiness.

BODY Firm, smooth, slightly viscous.

PALATE Deceptively delicate at first. Perfumy. Faint hint of fruity seaweed.
Then lightly waxy, becoming smoky. Dry.

FINISH Aromatic, smooth, appetizing.

SCORE **79**

OBAN 1980, Double Matured, Distillers Edition, 43 vol

Finished in Montilla fino wood.

COLOUR Amber.

NOSE Fragrant. Edible seaweed. Peaches. Very complex.

BODY Smooth, bigger.

PALATE Salty, nutty, peachy. Sweet in the middle, developing
notes of tobacco and seaweed.

FINISH The salt comes rolling back like an incoming tide.

SCORE **80**

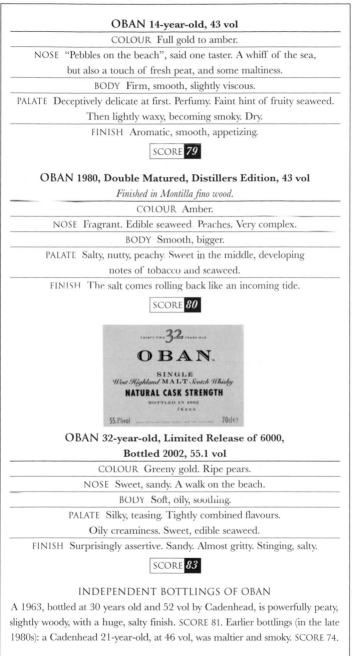

OBAN 32-year-old, Limited Release of 6000,
Bottled 2002, 55.1 vol

COLOUR Greeny gold. Ripe pears.

NOSE Sweet, sandy. A walk on the beach.

BODY Soft, oily, soothing.

PALATE Silky, teasing. Tightly combined flavours.
Oily creaminess. Sweet, edible seaweed.

FINISH Surprisingly assertive. Sandy. Almost gritty. Stinging, salty.

SCORE **83**

INDEPENDENT BOTTLINGS OF OBAN

A 1963, bottled at 30 years old and 52 vol by Cadenhead, is powerfully peaty,
slightly woody, with a huge, salty finish. SCORE 81. Earlier bottlings (in the late
1980s): a Cadenhead 21-year-old, at 46 vol, was maltier and smoky. SCORE 74.

PITTYVAICH

PRODUCER Diageo
REGION Highlands   DISTRICT Speyside (Dufftown)
SITE OF FORMER DISTILLERY
Dufftown, Banffshire, AB55 4BR

Bulldozed in 2002, after a short and unglamorous life, the industrial-looking distillery was built by Bell's in 1975. In the late 1980s, enthusiasts for single malts began to wonder whether the product would become available to them. Then independent bottler James MacArthur released a 12-year-old, revealing a perfumy, soft-pear house character. The same bottler then added a 14-year-old that more assertively pronounces its dry finish. A bottling of the same age from the Scotch Malt Whisky Society was similar, but seemed to have more spicy dryness on the nose. In 1991 there was finally an official bottling, at 12 years old, in United's Flora and Fauna series. This has all the other characteristics, plus a hefty dose of sherry.

HOUSE STYLE Fruity, oily, spicy, spirity.
After dinner – a Scottish grappa, so to speak.

PITTYVAICH 12-year-old, Flora and Fauna, 43 vol

COLOUR Deep amber red.

NOSE Sherryish, perfumy, pear skin.

BODY Light to medium. Firm. Dry.

PALATE Very sherryish. Assertive. Some malty chewiness. Vanilla.
Soft, sweet, pear-like fruitiness, moving to a spicy dryness.

FINISH Spicy, perfumy, intensely dry, lingering on the tongue.

SCORE 69

PORT ELLEN

PRODUCER Diageo
REGION Islay DISTRICT South Shore
SITE OF FORMER DISTILLERY Port Ellen, Isle of Islay, PA42 7AH
WEBSITE www.malts.com

WHICH WILL BE THE FINAL VINTAGE of this cult whisky? As stocks at the distillery diminish, and the fashionability of Islay soars, speculation mounts. Port Ellen is the rarest of Islay malts, despite a surprising number of independent bottlings. The distillery, near the island's main ferry port, was founded in 1825, substantially rebuilt and expanded during the boom years of the 1960s, then closed during the downturn in the 1980s. In the last two or three years, the modern parts of the distillery have been demolished, but the original pair of malt kilns have been preserved, complete with pagodas.

Adjoining the distillery is a modern maltings. The malt is supplied, in varying levels of peatiness, to all of the other Islay distilleries, including those which make a proportion of their own.

In 1995, Diageo started marketing whiskies from silent distilleries as The Rare Malts. These are vintage dated, so the number of bottles is determined by the amount of whisky held from a single year. In 1998, a 20-year-old Port Ellen was included in the range. In 2000, there was a further bottling of the same vintage at 22 years old. In order to vary the offerings, The Rare Malts had made it a rule not to feature the same distillery two years running. Such was the interest in the Port Ellen that it was decided to circumvent the rule. The Rare Malts selection ceased to include Port Ellen, which became a stand-alone Limited Edition. After three releases (*see overleaf*), of 6000 to 12,000 bottles each, the final vintage seemed nigh.

HOUSE STYLE Oily, peppery, salty, smoky, herbal. With smoked fish.

PORT ELLEN 1979, 22-year-old, Limited Edition Numbered Bottles, First Release 2001, 56.2 vol

COLOUR Solid, greeny gold. Bright, refractive.

NOSE Fresh. Bison grass. Cereal grain. Oily.

BODY Firm, nutty, malty.

PALATE Earthy. Peaty. Salty. Quite hard. Austere.

FINISH Pronounced salt. Dry smokiness. Intensely appetizing.

SCORE 92

PORT ELLEN 1978, 24-year-old, Limited Edition Numbered Bottles, Second Release 2002, 59.35 vol

COLOUR Lemony with golden hues.

NOSE Grassy and herbal. Dill, angelica, camomile.
A pleasant earthiness comes through.

BODY Tender.

PALATE Surprisingly smooth and sweet. A refreshing coolness.
Smokiness slowly emerges and hovers on menthol and vanilla.

FINISH Pleasantly dry and slowly dying.

SCORE 90

PORT ELLEN 1979, 24-year-old, Limited Edition Numbered Bottles, Third Release 2003, 56.2 vol

COLOUR Pale gold. Faint green tinge.

NOSE Herbal. Slightly sour. Seaweedy. Sea breezes.

BODY Soft, textured.

PALATE Edible seaweed. Salty flavours reminiscent of
some vermouths. Developing spicy notes.

FINISH Powerful, peppery, warming.

SCORE 91

PORT ELLEN 21-year-old, Anniversary Bottling, 58.4 vol

A rare "official" bottling, to celebrate 25 years of the maltings at Port Ellen.

COLOUR Bright gold.

NOSE Very medicinal, but clean and firm.

BODY Exceptionally oily, creamy.

PALATE Smooth and deceptively restrained at first, then the tightly
combined flavours emerge: bay leaves, parsley, peppercorns.

FINISH Slowly unfolding. Salty, smoky, oaky. Very warming. A subtlety and
complexity to which no aquavit or pepper vodka could quite aspire.

SCORE 83

ROSEBANK

PRODUCER Diageo
REGION Lowland   DISTRICT Central Lowlands
SITE OF FORMER DISTILLERY Falkirk, Stirlingshire, FK1 5BW
WEBSITE www.malts.com

IN 2002, THE QUEEN OPENED The Falkirk Wheel, a rotating lift to hoist boats between the Union canal and the restored Forth-Clyde canal. There had been hopes that the development of the canalside at Falkirk would include a tourist distillery to replace the silent Rosebank, but this prospect seems to have vanished.

Roses once bloomed on the banks of the Forth-Clyde canal, and a great deal of very early industry grew there. The Rosebank distillery may have had its origins as early as the 1790s. From the moment the canals lost business to the roads, the distillery's location turned from asset to liability. The road awkwardly bisected the distillery and as the traffic grew, it was difficult for trucks to drive in and out of the distillery. Rosebank was closed in 1993.

Rosebank's whisky at its best (i.e. not too woody) is as flowery as its name. It was the finest example of a Lowland malt, and was produced by triple distillation, in the Lowland tradition. It is a grievous loss.

HOUSE STYLE Aromatic, with suggestions of clover and camomile. Romantic. A whisky for lovers.

ROSEBANK 12-year-old, Flora and Fauna, 43 vol

This is a second version, released in 2003. It is a little drier and less lively than the first.

COLOUR Limey yellow.
NOSE Rosebank's typical camomile.
BODY Lightly creamy.
PALATE Flowery sweetness.
FINISH Mint imperials.
COMMENT Beginning to tire. Snatch a kiss while you can.

SCORE **76**

STRATHMILL

PRODUCER Diageo
REGION Highlands   DISTRICT Speyside (Strathisla)
ADDRESS Keith, Banffshire, AB55 5DQ
TEL 01542 885000   WEBSITE www.malts.com

GRAPES HAVE TO BE CRUSHED; grain has to be milled. The town of Keith must once have been a considerable grain-milling centre. The Glen Keith distillery was built on the site of a corn mill. Strathmill, as its name suggests, went one better. It was rebuilt from a corn mill, in 1891, when the whisky industry was having one of its periodic upswings. Three years later, it was acquired by Gilbey, of which Justerini & Brooks became a subsidiary through IDV (Diageo). Arguably, it has been in the same ownership for more than a century. Its whisky was for many years central to the Dunhill/Old Master blends, but does not seem to have been available as a single until a bottling of a lusciously sweet 1980 by the wine merchant chain, Oddbins, in 1993.

HOUSE STYLE The whisky world's answer to orange muscat. With dessert.

STRATHMILL 12-year-old, Flora and Fauna, 43 vol

COLOUR Lively gold.

NOSE Grassy and malty. With a delicate, floral touch. Clover. Orange peel.

BODY Smooth and flowing.

PALATE Sweet and fulfilling. Appealing freshness.
Honeycomb, orange. Hint of mint.

FINISH Drying on a resiny but soothing note.

SCORE 78

TALISKER

PRODUCER Diageo
REGION Highlands ISLAND Skye
ADDRESS Carbost, Isle of Skye, IV47 8SR
TEL 01478 614308
WEBSITE www.discovering-distilleries.com/www.malts.com VC

ALREADY VOLCANICALLY POWERFUL, Talisker has boosted its impact in recent years by adding new expressions. However many versions there may be, it remains a singular malt. It has a distinctively peppery character, so hot as to make one taster's temples steam. The phrase "explodes on the palate" is among the descriptions used for certain whiskies by blenders at UDV; surely they had Talisker in mind when they composed this. "The lava of the Cuillins" was another taster's response. The Cuillins are the dramatic hills of Skye, the island home of Talisker. The distillery is on the west coast of the island, on the shores of loch Harport, in an area where Gaelic is still spoken. The local industry was once tweed.

After a number of false starts on other sites, the distillery was established in 1831 and expanded in 1900. For much of its life, it used triple distillation, and in those days Robert Louis Stevenson ranked Talisker as a style on its own, comparable with the Islay and Livet whiskies. It switched to double distillation in 1928, and was partly rebuilt in 1960. The distillery uses traditional cooling coils – "worm tubs" – which can make for a fuller flavour than a modern condenser.

Some malt lovers still mourn the youthfully dry assertiveness of the eight-year-old version that was replaced by the current, more rounded version a couple of summers older. For a time, this was the only expression, but official bottlings have multiplied. As if to balance an equation, independent bottlings seem to have vanished.

HOUSE STYLE Volcanic. A winter warmer.

TALISKER 10-year-old, 45.8 vol

COLOUR Bright amber red.

NOSE Pungent, smoke-accented, rounded.

BODY Full, slightly syrupy.

PALATE Smoky, malty sweet, with sourness and a very big
pepperiness developing.

FINISH Very peppery, huge, long.

SCORE 90

TALISKER Natural Cask Strength, No Age Statement, Bottled 2000, 60 vol

Available at the distillery.

COLOUR Very bright. Yellow with an olive tinge.

NOSE Wild garlic. Blanched spinach with cracked black pepper.

BODY Oily.

PALATE Starts smoothly and has huge development toward earthy,
chive-like, seaweedy, medicinal notes.

FINISH Soft and smooth on the tongue, drying toward a late surge of salt,
ground white pepper and lactic acidity (ricotta cheese?)

SCORE 77

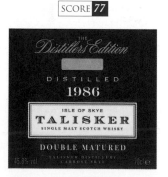

TALISKER "Double Matured", 1986, Distillers Edition, 45.8 vol

Finished in amoroso sherry wood.

COLOUR Orange.

NOSE Toffee, bitter chocolate, and toasted nuts, with late salt and pepper.

BODY Full, textured.

PALATE Toffeeish, then toasty. The richness of these flavours introduces a shock of contrast when the seaweed and pepper suddenly burst through.

FINISH Powerful salt and pepper.

SCORE **90**

TALISKER 1982, 20-year-old, 58.8 vol

COLOUR Gold, with green tinge.

NOSE Scorched earth. Harbour aromas. Seaweed.

BODY Medium to full. Firm.

PALATE Distant thunder. Seems to rumble and reverberate as the volcanic heat builds ever so slowly. Hot, slightly sour, peppery. Very tightly combined flavours, reluctant to unfurl. When they did, the earth moved.

FINISH Quite quick and sharp. A thunderflash.

SCORE **93**

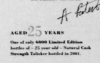

TALISKER 25-year-old, Bottled 2001, 59.9 vol

COLOUR Peachy, tan.

NOSE Warm. Minerally. A hint of sulphur.

BODY Quite rich.

PALATE Nutty, with a suggestion of artichoke. A touch of salt, then a burst of freshly milled pepper.

FINISH Volcanic. Reverberating.

SCORE **92**

TEANINICH

PRODUCER Diageo
REGION Highlands DISTRICT Northern Highlands
ADDRESS Alness, Ross-Shire, IV17 0XB
TEL 01463 872004 WEBSITE www.malts.com

THIS LESSER KNOWN NEIGHBOUR of Glenmorangie and Dalmore is beginning to develop a following for its big, malty, fruity, spicy whisky: not before time. Teaninich was founded in 1817, as an estate distillery, and later provided whisky for such well-known blends as VAT 69 and Haig Dimple. It gained a classic DCL still-house in the 1970s. The tongue-twisting name Teaninich (usually pronounced "tee-ninick", but some say "chee-ninick") began to be heard more widely in the 1990s, when the malt was bottled in the Flora and Fauna series. Three Rare Malts bottlings followed.

HOUSE STYLE Robust, toffeeish, spicy, leafy. Restorative or after dinner.

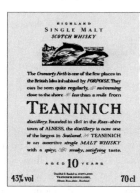

TEANINICH 10-year-old, Flora and Fauna, 43 vol

COLOUR Pale gold.

NOSE Big, fresh aroma. Fruity. Hints of apple. Smoky.

BODY Medium, rich.

PALATE Sweet and dry. Chocolate limes. Fruity. Remarkably leafy. Lightly peaty. Gradually warms up until it fairly sparks with flavour. Very appetizing.

FINISH Cilantro. Herbal. Rounded.

SCORE **74**

GETTING THE MOST OUT OF YOUR MALT

W HEN WE ENJOY DRINK, or food, we use all our senses: sight, smell, taste, and hearing. Do you listen to your food and drink? You do when you hear the steak sizzling in the pan, the whisky being poured from the bottle, or the clink of glasses.

Lovers of malt whisky want to enjoy to the full its subtleties of colour, its arousing bouquet, and its complex flavours. Malt lovers tend to dislike the cut-glass tumbler that is often regarded as the traditional whisky glass. The bevels in the glass may illuminate the colour of the whisky, but they also distort it. More important, the tumbler shape does a poor job of delivering aroma.

The size of the tumbler does accommodate ice, but a frozen tongue cannot taste properly. When the tumbler assumed its role, whisky was a hugely popular drink, but it had not yet inspired the connoisseurship it enjoys today.

Malt lovers prefer a brandy snifter, sherry copita, or something similar. These glasses were designed to showcase the special characteristics of noble and complex drinks. The growing connoisseurship of malts has led to the evolution of whisky glasses based on a similar, tulip-like shape.

Having tried every glass on the market, the author has observed that the tiniest variations in shape can make a huge difference in the delivery of aroma and flavour. Based on his experience, he has designed his own Whisky Connoisseur Glass, with spirits consultant Jürgen Deibel. The bowl of the glass has no decoration, so that the colour of the whisky can be appreciated to the full. The inward curve above the bowl holds in the aroma. Then the slight flare directs the bouquet to the nose. There is a lid to retain the aroma between sniffs and swallows.

THE QUESTION OF WATER

It is conceivable that the heroes of Scottish history drank their whisky neat; however, contrary to myth, today's Highlanders do not. "Half and half,

Sweet smell?
The successful shape is a variant of the copita.

with lots of water" is a common prescription. Some malt zealots do resist dilution – on principle. Others feel that the texture of the bigger, richer, sherryish malts is spoiled by water.

The problem is that neat whisky can numb the palate. This can be countered with a glass of water with which to chase down their whisky. In the whisky itself, even a drop of water, by disturbing the molecular composition of the whisky, can open the aromas and flavours. To avoid chlorine notes, bottled water (without carbonation) is preferred.

MALT WHISKY WITH FOOD

Anyone who enjoys a whisky after work, or in the early evening, is arguably treating it as an aperitif. A light, flowery, dryish dram best suits that purpose. Increasingly, some of the richer, creamier, more oaky malts are being offered after dinner.

Although there is no tradition of accompanying a meal with whisky, some malt lovers like to offer "the wine of Scotland". The first public manifestation of this was a whisky dinner organized by the author in the early 1990s, at the University of Pennsylvania's Museum of Anthropology and Archaeology.

The object was to help highlight the aromas and flavours of whisky by relating them to the tastes in the meal, which employed materials typically found in Scotland. It was a simple demonstration of possible affinities. The starter was smoked salmon marinated in the salty Oban and garnished with seaweed. The accompanying whisky was the lightly piney Isle of Jura, served in a small sherry copita. The main course was venison in a sauce made from Perthshire raspberries marinated in Blair Athol. This was served with the spicy Royal Lochnagar. The dessert was a butterscotch flan, flavoured with the honeyish Balvenie and served with the nutty Macallan 18-year-old.

Collaborations followed with Oregonian chef Christopher Zefiro (at The James Beard House, New York's shrine to gastronomy) and with French writer-cook Martine Nouet (in Scotland, initially at the Aberlour distillery). Nouet began to write a regular cookery column in *Whisky Magazine*. This publication has also run blindfold tastings to match malts with sushi, cheese, chocolate, and coffee. The materials in sushi – grain, fish, and seaweed – are superbly accompanied by some maritime malts. A sushi-and-whisky lunch, prepared by a former chef to the Emperor of Japan, was a highlight in a series of meals presented by Diageo.

The post-prandial cigar might well have been a smoky Lagavulin. In different company, it could be Dalmore's Cigar Malt – or Glenfiddich's Havana Reserve.

WHISKY SHOPS

Malt whisky is far easier to find today than it was when the first edition of this book was published 17 years ago. Some of the ground-breaking retailers in fact double as independent bottlers.

Among those, The Vintage House, of Old Compton Street, London, opened a tasting room in 2003. Its Soho neighbour, Milroy's, of Greek Street, pioneered this idea. Milroy's is now part of the La Réserve group. Visitors to London, travelling through Heathrow, Gatwick or Stansted airports, will find an excellent selection and knowledgeable staff at half a dozen specialist shops called Whiskies of the World. These are separate from the supermarket-style former duty-free shops.

In Scotland, people visiting Campbeltown or Islay by road might find Inverary a good place to break the journey – and visit Loch Fyne Whiskies. Such shops are institutions. The same is true of Park Avenue Liquors, in Manhattan. (The last is in fact not on Park Avenue but on Madison, between 40th and 41st).

BIBLIOGRAPHY & FURTHER INFORMATION

HISTORY
The Whisky Distilleries of the United Kingdom,
Alfred Barnard.
(Accounts of visits to distilleries. 1887 classic, with reprints in 1969, 1987, 2002, 2003)

The Making of Scotch Whisky,
John R. Hume and Michael S. Moss.
Canongate, 1981. Updated 2000. (Standard work)

The Scotch Whisky Industry Record, Charles Craig.
Index Publishing Limited, 1994. (Includes year-by-year chronology from 1494)

Scotch Whisky: A Liquid History, Charles MacLean.
Cassell, 2003. (Social history/commentary, by a whisky specialist)

REFERENCE
The Whisk(e)y Treasury,
Walter Schobert.
Neil Wilson Publishing, 2002. Originally published by Wolfgang Krüger Verlag, 1999. (A to Z lexicon of brand-owners, distilleries and industry terms)

The Scotch Whisky Industry Review (annual),
Alan S. Gray.
Sutherlands, Edinburgh.
(Industry statistics, financial analysis and commentary)

PRACTICAL
Appreciating Whisky,
Phillip Hills.
HarperCollins, 2000. Reprinted 2002. (The physiology, psychology and chemistry of taste)

Scotland and its Whiskies,
Michael Jackson.
Duncan Baird, 2001. (From the sea-spray to the scorched moorlands … treading the terroir that shapes the whiskies; with landscape photographer Harry Cory Wright)

The World Guide to Whisky,
Michael Jackson.
Dorling Kindersley, 1987. Reprints 1990, 1991, 1992, 1994, 1996, 1997. (The geography of the spirit – recognizing at first hand the qualities of Japanese, North American, and Irish whiskies alongside those of Scotland)

MAGAZINES & WEBSITES
Whisky Magazine
(Published in the United Kingdom)
www.whiskymag.com

Malt Advocate
(Published in the United States)
www.maltadvocate.com

Celtic Malts
(International news, issues and debates, among devotees. Online magazine)
www.celticmalts.com/default.htm

Ulf Buxrud is a Swedish computer entrepreneur and devotee of Macallan, whose personal website offers an extraordinary compilation of news, sources of reference, useful addresses, titles of publications, and general information of assistance to the whisky lover.
www2.sbbs.se/hp/buxrud/whisky.htm

For official websites devoted to particular malts, see distillery entries.

AUTHOR'S ACKNOWLEDGMENTS

Whatever I know about malts has been absorbed over decades, some of it directly from the glass; more from people who share my enthusiasm; yet more from those who make or market whisky. The diversity of their knowledge and opinions provide a broad foundation for my own, for which I take complete responsibility.

Although I keep notes of whiskies tasted in bars and restaurants, during distillery tours, and with my colleagues, that is an exercise in monitoring. The whiskies newly described and scored in this edition were sampled specifically for the book.

With more than a thousand tasting notes and scores, the gathering of samples was a massive task. For their generous time and effort in helping with this edition, I thank the following. If your name is not there, and should be, my apologies. I will put that right next time.

Pauline Agnew, Nick Andrews, Bridget Arthur, Elaine Bailey, Liselle Barnsley, Rachel Barrie, Michael Barton, Thierry Benitah, Bill Bergius, Jérôme Bordenave, David Boyd, Neil Boyd, Derek Brown, Lew Bryson, Lucy Byrne, Alec Carnie, Rick Christie, Neil Clapperton, Paula Cormack, Isabel Coughlin, Simon Coughlin, Andrew Crook, Jim Cryle, Bob Dalgarno, Joanne Doran, Lucy Drake, Jonathan Driver, Gavin J.P. Durnin, Anthony Edwards, Hans-Jürgen Ehmke, Kate Enis, Robert Fleming, John Glaser, Alan Gordon, Jim Gordon, Lesley Gracie, Heather Graham, George Grant, Alan S. Gray, Peter Greve, Natalie Guerin, Donald Hart, Deirdre Headon, Ian Henderson, Stuart Hendry, Robert Hicks, Sandy Hislop, Heather Hughes, David Hume, Brigid James, Richard Jones, Edward Kinsey, Kiran Kuma, Fred Laing, Stewart Laing, Christine Logan, Richard Lombard-Chibnall, Jim Long, Peter Luff, Bill Lumsden, Lorne Mackillop, Carla Masson, Fritz Maytag, Anthony McCallum-Caron, Jim McEwan, Frank McHardy, Douglas McIvor, Claire Meikle, Sue Metcalfe-Megginson, Marcin Miller, Euan Mitchell, Matthew Mitchell, Shuna Mitchell, Mike Miyamoto, Lindsay Morgan, Nicholas Morgan, Malcolm Mullin, Margaret Nicol, B.A. Nimmo, Rebecca Painter, The Patel Family, Richard Paterson, Lucy Pritchard, Annie Pugh, John Ramsay, Stuart Ramsay, Kevin Ramsden, Kirsty Reid, Mark Reynier, Rebecca Richardson, Dave Robertson, Geraldine Roche, Dominic Roskrow, Colin Ross, Fabio Rossi, Colin Scott, Jacqui Seargeant, Catherine Service, Euan Shand, Sarah Sherlock, Raj Singh, Sukhinder Singh, David Stewart, David Stirk, Elizabeth Stubbs, Kier Sword, Andrew Symington, Elodie Teissedre, Jens Tholstrup, Graeme Thomson, Margaret Mary Timpson, Hide Tokuda, Robin Torrie, Diana Tu, Robin Tucek, Simon Tuite, The Urquhart Family, Alistair Walker, Louise Waller, Ian Weir, Amy Westlake, Alan Winchester, Arthur Winning, Gordon Wright, Kate Wright, Vanessa Wright.

Countless other people in the industry have helped me over the years, and their assistance is much appreciated.

Dorling Kindersley would like to thank Pamela Marmito and Gary Werner for editorial assistance, and Ritzenhof Cristal for Michael Jackson's tasting glass (*see p. 141*), which is available from De Hoeksteen Projects b.v./www.hoeksteen-glasses.nl.

All photography by Ian O'Leary except Diageo plc (12, 20, 26, 27, 31, 35, 37, 41, 42, 45), Paul Harris (46), Steve Gorton (1, 2–3, 5, 141).